Forty Days a...

Yemen

A Journey to Tarim, the City of Light

↑ *Palm tree in the Ba'Alawi square,*
seemingly growing out of a wall

Ethar El-Katatney

Ta-Ha Publishers Ltd.

© Ta-Ha Publishers Ltd. 1410 AH/2010 CE

First Published in March 2010 by

Ta-Ha Publishers Ltd
Unit 4, The Windsor Centre
Windsor Grove, West Norwood
London SE27 9NT
UK

Website: www.taha.co.uk
E-mail: sales@taha.co.uk

Text and Photography by: Ethar El-Katatney
General Editor: Dr. Abia Afsar-Siddiqui
Book Design by: Shakir Abdulcadir opensquares.co.uk
Cover Design by: Saleha Atewala

A catalogue record of this book is available from the British Library

ISBN-13: 978-1-84200-119-6

Printed and bound by: Imak Ofset

In the Name of Allah, the Most Gracious, the Most Merciful

All praise be to Allah the Almighty, and blessings and peace be upon our Master the Prophet Muhammad, his family and Companions.

This diary, which is the first written work of my dear blessed Ethar (who is like a daughter to me), is sincere in its emotional outpourings, brilliant in its ideas and profound in its meanings. Its language is spontaneous, coming from a pure heart, nurtured by loving Allah the Almighty, with a willingness to draw near to Him, and insightfully working towards looking after the planet through a harmonious interaction between humans, animals, plants and even inanimate objects, on the basis of good neighbourly love, and utilisation of God's gifts to man: intellect and knowledge gleaned through learning.

Ethar graduated with distinction from the A.U.C, and was brought up in a family that provided her with a gracious livelihood and an interest in learning. Her mother is a physician – also the daughter of well-known physician Dr. Husain Ibrahim al-Azghal – who memorises the Holy Qur'an by heart. Her father Mr. Kamal Katatney, is a businessman and an engineer by profession.

In the course of the forty days she spent in Tarim, the city of scholars and saints, where she lived a life of religious learning integrated with remembrance of God and spirituality, she noted down her experiences.

Amongst what attracted me to this diary is the sincerity of her expression, from a mind which is in a state of total submission, yet can be critical to the point of being provocative, and a spirit which is spiritually intoxicated and consumed by love, and with a heart which flutters with joy and is also contrite with sadness.

In the diary, there is an attempt of bridging a wrongly-assumed gap between religion and life, another between knowledge and practice, and another between action and forethought.

I also found, while reading excerpts from the diary, honest spontaneous messages addressed to those responsible for directing the Islamic discourse, others addressed to those leading contemporary education, and others addressed to those contributing to directing the society and decision making in the world. I really hope such experience of an intelligent girl is to be well read.

May Allah bestow upon this diary and its writer His blessing and pleasure in this world and the hereafter, and inspire her with whatever is good for her and the world, for He has power over everything. Ameen.

Ali bin Abdur-Rahman al-Jifri

Introduction

Al salam 'alaykum wa rahmatu Allahu wa barakatu.
May the peace and blessings of Allah be upon you.

In 2008, I travelled to Tarim, a small town in Yemen, to attend the annual summer *Dowra*, an intensive forty day course in traditional Islamic sciences. As one of my teachers said, those of us who were there got the opportunity to study blessed topics in a blessed city. It was a whirlwind, life-changing forty days which impacted me greatly.

Life in our world today has become so intense and busy that we sometimes feel like we need a 'disconnect and recharge' button. Tarim was that place for me, where spirituality is in the air and where I felt my soul could breathe. A place where I could recharge my spiritual batteries, connect with my Creator, learn more about myself, and return to the world rejuvenated - though there will always be a part of me that yearns to go back.

Tarim is a small town nestled between enormous mountains in the Hadhramaut Valley of eastern Yemen. An important locus of Islamic learning, Tarim is the theological, juridical and academic centre of Yemen, and has long been considered a beacon of Islamic knowledge, distinguished for producing numerous Islamic scholars. The Islamic Educational, Scientific and Cultural Organisation (ISESCO) chose Tarim as the Capital of Islamic Culture 2010.

It is estimated that one in three Tarimis are *sayyids*, descendants of the Prophet Muhammad ﷺ, making Tarim the city with the highest concentration of them anywhere in the world.

About Yemen, Sayyiduna Abu Hurayra 🕮 narrates that the Messenger of Allah 🕮 said:

"The people of Yemen have come to you. They are tender-hearted and more delicate of soul. The capacity to understand (*fiqh*) is of the Yemenis and wisdom is that of the Yemenis." (*Sahih al-Bukhari and Sahih Muslim*)

During the caliphate of Sayyiduna Abu Bakr 🕮, Tarim was the only Yemeni city which paid the annual *zakat* during the wars of apostasy. In response, the caliph made this *du'a* for Tarim: "Allah make plentiful its water, and make it cultivated till the Day of Judgement, and may the Righteous blossom in its lands as plants blossom from water."

This book was written while I was out there. I've tried my best to recount the experience as it was, though of course my account by no means does it justice. The experience needed someone who could wax poetically over it, and unfortunately I was not up to the task. Because of time constraints and our intensive schedule, I wasn't as articulate and thorough as I could have been, so forgive me if some entries seem choppy.

Writing up my experiences took up a lot more time than I thought it would when I began, so I hope it is beneficial to those of you who were with me, those of you who are thinking of travelling to Tarim, and those of you who want to know what life is like in a place where Islam is truly a way of life.

Any mistakes are completely my own and if you were with me on this Dowra, please do let me know if I've misquoted someone or gotten something incorrect. It was an honour to meet you all and please forgive me if I somehow offended you or caused you any kind of distress.

One last note: this book is in no way affiliated with Dar al-Mustafa, Dar al-Zahra or anyone of the Dowra administration. It is simply an account of my journey and my reflections.

I'll end in the way the Dowra administration has been answering my e-mails to them for the past three years:
Please overlook my shortcomings, and keep me in your *du'a*s.

Wasalaam,
Ethar

↑ *Pigeons sitting in the shade of a window in a deserted house*

Bism Allah

Bism Allah Al-Rahman Al-Raheem.
In the Name of Allah, Most Gracious, Most Merciful.

My first diary entry for what I hope will be a life-changing experience for me, one I have been looking forward to for three years. I'm off to Yemen today for the Dowra, a forty day intensive Islamic 'summer school', for lack of a better term. Insha'Allah we will be focusing on three aspects: knowledge, spiritual wayfaring, and *da'wah* (calling to Islam). Dar al-Mustafa, where the classes will be held, is one of the most respected traditional Islamic learning institutions in the world.

It is located in Tarim, Hadhramaut, a town that is known as the Daughter of Madinah; a place where time stood still. People say that when you're there, you feel as if you've travelled back in time to the days of the beloved Prophet Muhammad ﷺ.

← *Typical houses of the area surrounded by mountains*

I'm nervous and apprehensive about being thrown in the deep end of a culture which, although similar to my own (Egyptian), is still strange in many ways. From the *niqab* (face veil) that has to be worn at all times in a segregated society, to waking up at 3am, it's all going to be a brand new experience. Why did I decide to go? Because, as Prophet Muhammad ﷺ said:

"Seeking knowledge is the duty of every Muslim. It will enable you to be your own friend in the desert, your mainstay in solitude. It will be your companion in loneliness, your guide to happiness, your sustainer in misery, your adornment when you are amongst people and your arrow against your enemies. Whoever goes out in search of knowledge is on the path of Allah until returning." (*Ibn Abdal-Barr*)

Also:

"Whoever decides to relocate solely to study sacred knowledge is forgiven before even setting out." (*Al-Tirmidhi*)

So my intention for going is:

نويت التعلم والتعليم، والتذكر والتذكير، والنفع والإنتفاع، والإفادة والاستفادة،
والحث على التمسك بكتاب الله، وسنة رسوله، والدعاء الى الهدى، والدلالة على الخير
ابتغاء وجه الله ومرضاته وقربه وثوابه سبحانه وتعالى

"I intend learning and teaching; reminding myself and reminding others; benefitting myself and benefitting others; encouraging people to hold fast to the Book of Allah and the Sunnah of the Messenger of Allah ﷺ; calling people to guidance; guiding people to good, and [in doing all this] seeking the countenance, pleasure, nearness and the reward of Allah Most High." (*Imam 'Abd-Allah ibn 'Alawi al-Haddad*)

A student of knowledge, said Imam al-Shafi'i, needs five things - humility, intention, patience, a craving for knowledge and estrangement. I'm sure I have three of those things and here's hoping I can cultivate my humility and patience.

Bism Allah.

Day 1: Sanaa

I have just landed in Yemen and my first impression is joy at the incredible weather. 20 degrees is a welcome break from 35 degree Cairo. But more than that, the air seems incredibly pure and still. I know that doesn't make sense, but that's what it feels like; the atmosphere lacks the vibrancy and fast pace of Cairo.

← *A short distance from Sanaa airport*

My flight got in at 2am and my connecting flight to Seiyun leaves at 8am. A friend of the family kindly invited my family and I to their home and it turns out that Yemeni hospitality eclipses Egyptian hospitality. (My mother, sister and brother are staying in Tarim too, though they're not part of the Dowra group.) The house smells of *bukhoor* (incense) and reminds me of Saudi Arabia's Abd El Samad El Qorashi (a famous incense chain). And the dates taste as good as the ones in Makkah too!

On the way to the house, I realise that *everyone* is chewing *Qat* (a marijuana-like drug which is part of the culture here) and that they're armed. Boys as young as fifteen are carrying heavy artillery and our host shrugs and tells us that that's the norm in Sanaa. Oh, and that daggers do not count as weaponry, since they are simply decoration. Even our host is armed with a silver gun. And wearing a suit jacket over the *jalabiya* (a white dress) seems to be the dress code for men.

Sanaa is so, so quiet. Perhaps because it's 3am, but regardless, the lack of people is strange. Houses are all one or two storey buildings and they're all made of unpainted bricks. Which is why when we came across one of the most beautiful mosques I've seen, President Saleh's mosque, one that cost millions of dollars to build, it seemed all the more beautiful for its uniqueness. I feel like I've stepped back in time. Until I see a billboard advertising Ragheb Alama's new album (a Lebanese singer). Sigh.

And now I hear the first *adhan* (prayer call) of Fajr. And a rooster crowing. Better get a couple of hours of sleep before I have to get up and continue the last leg of my trip.

Day 1 (Cont'd): Six-hour Drive

Well, that was definitely an experience. Today may well have been one of the longest days of my life.

We woke up at 6am, as our host told us, and were at the airport at 7am, only to be told that we were too late, and that the flight had been overbooked so they had given away our tickets. Ouch. Luckily (or so it seemed at the time), we ran into a group of foreigners who definitely looked Dowra-like. We told the organiser we were also headed to Dar al-Mustafa so he took our tickets and told us he would try and book us on a flight to Al-Rayaan (also known as Makalla). From there we could take a car to Tarim, as we would have done once we had landed in Seiyun. Both flights were an hour long and so we (wrongly) assumed that the car ride would be the same, approximately thirty minutes. Wrong. The car trip from Al-Rayaan airport to Tarim took us over SIX hours. By the time we got to Tarim it had been almost twenty-four hours since we'd left our house at Cairo.

The six hours in the hot car were not exactly fun. But looking on the bright side:

- Al-Rayaan is on the coast, so we got to see the beautiful sea as we landed.
- I got to see camels grazing in the midst of greenery and not to the backdrop of a desert.
- We stopped at a shady looking rest-stop and sat in a family room - a small window-less room with a carpet - where we ate chicken with rice Yemeni style, with our hands.
- We drove up a huge mountain. An incredible, incredible, scary experience. The road was literally built into the mountain and we were so high up my ears were popping. And then when we reached the top, we drove all the way to the end of the mountaintop.
- When we finally drove back down the mountain, we came across a valley called Al-'Ain, which is filled with literally thousands of palm trees; a sight I will never forget.
- I got to see *Qat*. I wrote a research paper about it in university and couldn't believe that it really was as widespread as I'd read. Our driver stopped on the way to pick up a bag of *Qat* and chewed it all the way as leisurely as if he was chewing a stick of gum and not a drug. You see, according to him, it's a *monabeh* (makes you alert), not a drug.

↓ *Looking down at Al-Rayaan from the plane*

*→↓ Travelling down
the mountain*

↓ *En-route
to Tarim*

And now we are in Tarim, in the valley of Hadhramaut. The name literally translates into "death has arrived". Someone once told me, Hadhramaut is where people come to die - not physically die but as in erasing everything about them that is tied to this world. My heart seems lighter as I take in the view and breathe in the air. I can't help feeling that today has made me appreciate being in Tarim even more and that the hardship endured to get here makes the upcoming experience all the more precious in my eyes.

I've been wanting to come to Tarim since 2006, and even though I was accepted in the 2006 Dowra and the 2007 one, circumstances arose and I couldn't attend either one. Subhan Allah, I wasn't accepted this year and only got in when a sister backed out at the last minute. So all these events combined make me all the more determined to make use of every single minute I have here.

Day 2: Material Life

I just woke up and it's 10:30am. Not very good considering that in a couple of nights I will have to be waking up at 3am (insha'Allah).

So for this morning's entry, I wanted to reflect a bit on how attached I've become to 'stuff'. There's this song by Zain Bhikha I love titled, "Can't take it with you (when you go)" and I've always loved it because it shows how material we've become.

↑ *This is the view outside my apartment window*

Houses in Yemen are very, very basic and look unfinished, as if they are half-built. Most are made of mud bricks, which are then painted over (as far as I understand) with something that makes them not melt in the rain. You feel that the houses are not only environmentally friendly, but part of the earth. And because – apart from the main roads – the roads are unpaved, dusty and rocky, you feel like you are in a very un-urban place.

Being so close to nature is new to me and definitely makes you more aware of how small you are in the grand scheme of things. In Egypt, the only reason anyone would have a house like the ones here would be because they were too poor to build a better one. But here, I think another reason is because for many people, houses are just places where they sleep and live, they don't need to be incredible on the inside and outside - the need to show off isn't there. The physical environment in Tarim also forces many people into an ascetic mode of living.

→ *Houses just outside Tarim*

The flat I'm in right now consists of two small bedrooms, two tiny airport size bathrooms, one empty room (which I presume is for entertaining guests) and a kitchen. Each bedroom has two mattresses with a pillow, and only one of the bathrooms has a proper toilet; the other is just a hole in the floor. The kitchen has a refrigerator, cooker (gas, though - don't think I've seen one of those in ages) and a semi-automatic washing machine. Because of the heat, there's an air conditioner in each bedroom (alhamdulillah!) but other than that the apartment is bare. No knick-knacks, no curtains, no useless things everywhere. And you know what? It's enough.

Sure, I've realised how much I depend on 'stuff' - ("Oh, I need a mirror to tie my *hijab*. Oh, how can I hang my *abayas* (long black simple dresses) with no hangers or closet?" etc.) but for the most part I relish this experience.

I've only been here a day, but I can already see that life here is so much simpler. The constant roaring in my ears that I always have back home (partially due to traffic - I haven't heard one car here), the constant drive to do this and this and this is simply non-existent. Just because the place is so simple. I get up, I pray, and I feel like I can take my time. I don't have to hurriedly get dressed, drive to work at breakneck speed, stopping only to pick up a sandwich, go to work, finish work, and head off to evening classes at university before trudging back home and doing it all again the next day.

At 10pm here, there's no one in the streets, which makes it easier to wake up for Fajr. Internet access is minimal, and even then Facebook, my biggest waste of time, is blocked. There's even something to be said for dressing the same (women in black *abayas* and *niqabs* and men in white *jalabiyas*) - the time wasted matching clothes and getting dressed simply becomes redundant. Of course, this doesn't mean I'm going to want to give up Facebook forever or dress the same way forever, but just that I understand the allure.

I've already fallen in love with this place. And with the Al-Rabie milk.

Day 2 (Cont'd): Dar al-Zahra

I spent the day today finishing up some work. Not the most productive use of my time here, but at least now I'm done with it.

Around Maghrib time, our neighbours came up to greet us, and what do you know? One of them is Egyptian! She very kindly offered to take us to Dar al-Zahra, which is the female version of Dar al-Mustafa, and I immediately took her up on the offer, since I hadn't yet met anyone. Dar al-Mustafa is named after the Prophet Muhammad ﷺ (one of his names is Mustafa, the chosen), and Dar al-Zahra is named after his daughter, Fatima al-Zahra ؏.

Dar al-Zahra is beautiful. We're not allowed to take pictures inside, but basically, imagine a building with a hole right down the middle. The hole is a courtyard, which airs the whole place out, and is where some classes are held, so you can see the sky directly. There's another courtyard on the other side, and both remind me of the mosque of Prophet Muhammad ﷺ, where the domes slide open to air the mosque.

To the right side of the main courtyard is the *musallah* (prayer area), and the rest of the building is made up of dorms and classrooms. During prayer time, everyone prays in congregation, and everyone wears a *kamees*, which is the traditional prayer gown tied behind the head.

↑ *Dar al-Zahra, the university and dorms for female students*

I got a small tour of the place and I met some of the women who were studying there. It will never cease to amaze me when I meet people from literally the other side of the world who give up their lives to come, live and study in a place that is so alien to their culture. Unlike what you may think, students aren't just Arabs or Indonesians; I met people from Britain, Kenya and Singapore.

Subhan Allah there are so, so many people studying there. There was a class being held when we came in, and as a rough estimate, there were at least two hundred women listening attentively. After the lecture, I finally ran into some of the other Dowra participants, who are staying in a house nearby. Four of them I'd already met before; they were with me in last year's *Rihla*.[1] It's such a small world and I was so happy to meet them again.

I'm thinking of moving in with the rest of the Dowra sisters rather than staying with my family. I mean, I see my family every day, but how often am I going to get a chance to experience the *ukhuwa* (sisterhood)?

---

1   The *Rihla* (journey) is an annual programme organised by the Deen Intensive Foundation, a North American initiative that seeks to preserve and propagate the core sacred sciences of traditional Islam. They organise intensive summer programmes in America, Spain, Morocco, Madinah and Makkah, where the students get to visit sacred locations and be taught by great shaykhs such as Shaykh Abdullah bin Bayyah and Shaykh Hamza Yusuf. I was blessed to have attended the 2007 Rihla in Madinah and Makkah.

Day 3: The Habayeb

How to describe today? I write for a living, but I'm having difficulty finding words to describe what today was like for me. Basically, all we did was visit some Westerners who live here and the *hababas* who will insha'Allah be giving the lectures. (The words *habib* and *hababa* [for a woman] are used to refer to scholars who are descendants of Prophet Muhammad ﷺ.) But in reality, the visits were so much more.

The first thing you realise when you meet the *hababas* is how much *haya* they have. *Haya* is loosely translated as modesty, but the word doesn't really cover the meaning it has in Arabic. They have *haya* not only in the way they dress, but in the way they talk and interact. The *hababas* reminded us of how lucky we were to be chosen to come here and of the importance of renewing our *niya* (intention) all the time.

The people here are *so* sincere. There aren't any of the social games that we play back home, where being friendly and genuine is perceived as a weakness. Everyone is so generous, so hospitable and so welcoming. The trip is so cheap (only $700) because none of the teachers or members of the Dowra administration are getting paid - they are doing this because they genuinely want us to learn and benefit. Here, you know that what you see is what you get; nothing is complicated because there's nothing to gain from being aloof and detached.

The normal way to greet people here is to make a movement to kiss their hand and then bring your hand to your heart or mouth and really kiss their hand if they are old and/or a scholar. I'm starting to get used to it and I think it's a beautiful sign of respect. The fact that I'm talking about kissing someone's hand so normally is an example of how the atmosphere here changes you. For example, I would rarely call anyone back home 'sister' or 'brother'- I'd feel it was kind of corny, but here it comes naturally.

↑ *Habib Ali's door which says 'Alive in our Hearts' and 'Allah'; made in plasticine by Habib Ali's daughter.*

The houses are all as simple as I imagined them to be, even the houses of the *habayeb*. Sparsely furnished, the houses all have the bare essentials and no more.

It's incredible how spiritual the place is and how life revolves around the prayers and not vice versa. Too often back home I find myself slotting prayers into time between work tasks and finishing them hurriedly. Here, prayers are a big chunk of the day and no one gets up immediately after them — everyone sits to make *dhikr* (remembrance of Allah) and *du'a* (supplication).

It's so, so hot here. It's hotter than Cairo by only a few degrees, but somehow it's a different kind of heat, an oppressive one. I am dehydrated all the time and it got me thinking about how we take all the modern appliances of our daily lives for granted. I mean, the air conditioner was only invented recently; before it, people lived in this heat normally. But it's good to endure a little tribulation. Our lives back home are so comfortable that we've become complacent, taking all the blessings we have for granted. A little discomfort makes you grateful for what you have and teaches you patience.

It was wonderful to meet the Western sisters who are studying in Tarim. Again, like I said before, it will never cease to amaze me how they can pack up and leave everything they know to come to somewhere that is so different from their home to study Islam. They greeted us singing the song the people in Yathrib (which later became Madinah) sang when the Prophet Muhammad ﷺ arrived there, *Tala'al badru 'alayna* (The moon has risen above us), and it was an honour.

While we were there, we were given us a short *dars* (lecture) by a female scholar. It's amazing to see and meet real women scholars, and it proves wrong the misconception that there aren't any real ones. One of the most profound things she told us was that the people who are close to Allah worry so much about wasting time that they call themselves to account for every breath they spend - how many of us wonder about how we spend our day, let alone each breath?

I went to the Dowra house today and I met the rest of the Dowra participants. Mash'Allah they come from so many different countries - the UK, the US, Bulgaria, Australia and even Brunei. The feeling of camaraderie in the house is so evident it's almost tangible. When the time comes to eat, everyone eats together from the same plate. And on that note, the food here tastes *so* good. Everything - the tea, the cakes, the bread, the tuna, the grilled chicken. Maybe it's partly because everything is fresh and natural here, but I'm sure part of it is due to the *barakah* (blessings) of Tarim. Today was a wonderful day. I haven't felt so at peace in a long time. And we haven't even started yet. Tomorrow morning at 3am, insha'Allah, the Dowra begins. *Tawakaltu 'ala Allah.*

Day 4: First Day of Classes

Today was the first day of classes and now I understand why very few Dowra students have attempted to put down in words what the experience is like. Words are really not adequate enough to convey the experience - like what was said in a class today, *zawq* (taste) must be felt, it cannot be conveyed. Honey and sugar are both sweet, but how can you describe the difference to someone who hasn't tasted either?

But another reason I'm sure no one has written extensively about the experience is that they're simply too tired! At the end of the day everyone is so exhausted that it's hard to even attempt to be as articulate and eloquent as you need to be to describe the experience. But I'll try my best and insha'Allah, I'll dedicate half an hour of my day to my entries. Today, I'll write about the day and insha'Allah, I'll elaborate more about the schedule in further entries.

The day started out with *Tahajjud* (night prayers) and *dhikr* before Fajr prayer. Subhan Allah I am able to concentrate and focus so much more on prayer when I feel that I have 'prepared' for it. I didn't just get up and stand in a corner and take five minutes out of my day; I made *wudu'* (ablution), walked to Dar al-Zahra, prayed the greeting of the mosque and recited my *wird* (litany), all before praying, and even then it was in *jama'a* (congregation).

After praying and doing the *dhikr*, all the sisters get up for *musafaha*: the imam gets up first and the first person to shake her hand stands next to her. Then the next person shakes both their hands and stands next to them. In this way, we all shake each other's hands. It sounds a bit strange, but it really 'cultivates' a sense of community and, for some reason, it really makes me smile. Plus, there's a hadith (Prophetic saying) that goes:

"When two Muslims shake hands, their sins fall to the ground, as leaves of the tree fall to the ground." (*Al-Tabarani*)

We then had our first class with Habib Umar ibn Hafiz (the head of Dar al-Mustafa) in his house studying Imam al-Haddad's *The Lives of Man*. I saw Habib Umar walking to the mosque, and subhan Allah his face is so peaceful and at ease. That's something that all the *habayeb* have here - their gaze is utterly serene and they have faces that seem divinely illuminated.

The best way I can put it is like this: imagine the look in a child's eyes to whom you've just given candy. And then the look in an adult's eyes who has so much to do and doesn't really like dealing with you. Visualising it? See how the subtle nuances in a person's gaze speak volumes? Now, the *habayeb*'s eyes are so much closer to a child's than an adult burdened with worldly cares - without guile, honest and content, only of course without the naivety and unawareness of the world around them children have.

↓ *Attending a lecture in Habib Umar's house*

Which makes it all the harder that we can't really *see* them. I mean, the Dowra team have provided us with all the equipment necessary to engage in the lecture - a TV and radio that provide audio and video, but of course it's not the same as actually sitting right in front of the shaykhs and being in their presence.

Basically, how it works is that we sit in a lecture room in Dar al-Zahra and have a TV in front of us broadcasting video and a radio broadcasting audio from the classes in Dar al-Mustafa - one channel Arabic, one channel English. In Habib Umar's house it's the same thing only we don't need a radio, just a microphone.

After the first class, I moved into the Dowra dormitory. True, the apartment I was staying in with my family was *much* more comfortable and sharing a flat with three people is easier than sharing a house with almost thirty women but I'm glad I moved in. I'm glad because a big part of the Dowra is the *ukhuwa*, and another is enduring difficulties and learning to be patient.

I've lived in a dormitory before, but it was in Birmingham in England, and there we each had our own bedroom and bathroom, and only shared one communal kitchen, which we never used since we ate out all the time. Plus, someone came to clean, so I've never had 'kitchen duty' or chores to do. Basically, I've never shared such close quarters with other women, and my knowledge of doing so is limited to sharing a bedroom with my sister when we were children and what I've seen on *America's Next Top Model*!

The house is really big and there are five or six of us in each room. It sounds really harsh when I say that each room is equipped with only five mattresses but in reality it's not at all that tough. Some rooms have marble tiles and others have vinyl flooring, and all of them have a small night light so if some people want to sleep and others don't, everyone is happy since it's not too dark or too light.

There's also an air conditioner and two fans in each room, so the room doesn't get too hot (still hot though), and there are no curtains which means we take our morning naps in full daylight (and I've always been the kind of person who needs complete and utter darkness to sleep, and even pulls the curtains shut at night). But after a long day I could probably be sleeping on the floor and still be happy, and the truth is the moment I put my head on my pillow I'm out like a light. But it's definitely not my room at home and it's going to be hard getting used to living out of a suitcase.

My roommates are pretty diverse. One is a British convert, one is an African-American convert from Seattle, one is British of Somalian descent, and the last is also British but of Yemeni/Omani descent. And then there's me, Saudi born and Egyptian raised. So it's pretty cool getting to know everyone.

Anyway, after Dhuhr prayer we all got our books, schedules and notebooks and I was so excited - I guess the nerd inside me still lives on!

After 'Asr prayer, we had *Al-Rawha* with Habib Umar - he has this really joyful laugh, by the way, just like Habib Ali has a beautiful smile - which is a class we have every day that talks about spiritual issues/disciplining the self.

Then we had a class after Maghrib prayer and one after 'Isha prayer. The two classes really made me think about an important issue, intentions, which I'll try and talk about in a separate entry. Tomorrow I'll also try and talk more about the classes and the schedule.

Oh, after 'Isha the Dar al-Zahra administration had a welcoming session for us, which was really nice of them. I got asked to introduce myself and how I found Tarim, as well as translate my roommate Lara's story about how she converted to Islam (she's the British one). It was kind of scary but alhamdulillah, I think we did ok.

Day 5: Intentions

The day hasn't started yet, so before it does I wanted to write this entry on *niya*. Intention has always been something I have struggled with and yesterday I was reminded of its importance in two classes.

In one class, we're studying *Imam Nawawi's Forty Hadith* and the first one talks about how actions are by intention - that what you do is not as important as why you did it. There are three types of people - those who do things purely for the sake of Allah, those who do things for the sake of Allah and other reasons, and those who do things purely for reasons other than Allah. I fall squarely into the second category and I'm honest enough to admit it. I am never, ever sure of my intentions.

In our second class, we began reading *The Beginning of Guidance* by Imam al-Ghazali, and on the very first page, I read:
"You should be sure that, if in your quest for knowledge your aim is competition, showing off, surpass[ing] your fellows, to attract people's attention to yourself, and to stockpile these worldly vanities, then [...] your bargain is dead loss, your trading without profit."

And then about the people who fall into the second category:
"[He is] aware of that ultimate truth [that his intentions aren't pure] and in his heart has some perception of the worthlessness of his condition and the vileness of his aim."

The first quote resonated with me, and the second one *is* me.

I've struggled with intentions for the last couple of years. At one stage, I got so scared of falling into *riya'* (ostentation that leads to hypocrisy) that I actually stopped performing a lot of good things that I did, just to cancel out the possibility that my motives may not be as pure as I hoped. I eventually learned that it was wrong to do so. One of the verses that scares me most in the Qur'an says: *"Say: shall we tell you of those who lost most in respect of their deeds? Those whose efforts have been wasted in this life, while they thought that they were acquiring good by their works?"* (Surat al-Kahf 18:103-104)

The following verse answers that they are "those who deny the Signs of their Lord and the fact of their having to meet Him." For me though, the verse scares me because likewise, if you're doing all these good deeds with intentions that aren't pure, they might not be accepted. Elsewhere in the book, Imam al-Ghazali continues: "If people really judged objectively, they would realise that it is only people's hypocrisy which is the motive of most of their intellectual pursuits and acts of Worship, not to mention their customary activities; and this hypocrisy renders their acts of no avail."

I feel that these mentions of *niya* were reminders for me, on my first day on this Dowra, to refocus and restate my intentions, and to work as hard as I can to make sure they are as pure as possible. And that also relates to this book as well. Stating your intention helps you focus on it, so for the record, I'm working on this diary to:

1 Provide a glimpse into a life that many think could not possibly exist in this day and age; a life that I think is similar to what life was like hundreds of years ago - with added amenities, of course. A life that I think highlights the best things about being a Muslim, things that if everyone implemented the image of Islam and Muslims in the world would be very different.

2 Help anyone who is thinking of coming here - to show them what the experience is like. I know I would have loved to have something like this to read before I came here.

3 Be a reminder for me and everyone with me on this Dowra of our experience here and the amazing things we did and saw. I used to have a scrapbook when I was a child where I used to stick everything I could get my hands on in it. But truly, taking mental 'snapshots' and remembering them by writing them down is much better. So I'm writing down our experiences to give us a 'spiritual boost' when we go back to our lives and ultimately begin forgetting what it was like to be here.

And since, as Prophet Muhammad ﷺ said:
"God loves a servant who when performing a task does so skilfully." (Al-Bayhaqi)

I will try my best to write faithfully in this diary every day and to recount our experiences to the best of my ability, insha'Allah.

Day 5 (Cont'd): Schedule

I feel as if I've been here for so long, though in reality it's been less than a week. Subhan Allah. As promised, here is our schedule:

Saturday – Wednesday:
3:15-4:50am: Tahajjud & Fajr
5-5:45: Qur'an recitation on Saturday, Sunday, Monday
Class on Tuesday and Wednesday
6-10: Breakfast & qayloola (morning nap)
10:30-11:45: Class
12-3pm: Lunch & Dhuhr & rest
3:15-5: 'Asr & Al-Rawha
5:15-6:15: Review & Maghrib
6:30-7:30: Class
7:30-8: 'Isha
8-9: Class
9:30: Dinner

On Thursday, we don't have classes. Instead, we have the *khatam* (*du'a* for finishing reading the Qur'an), a pool gathering (!), local *ziyaras* (visits) and a *mawlid*[2], which I'm really looking forward to. On Friday we only have two classes, the rest of the day we have *ziyaras*. Classes are held in Habib Umar's house, and only the *rawha* and *seerah* (Prophetic history) classes are held at Dar al-Zahra.

These are the main topics we are studying and our teachers:
- *The Lives of Man* (Habib Umar)
- *Seerah* (Habib Umar)
- *Da'wah* (Habib Ali)
- *Da'wah* in the West (Habib Ali)
- The Beginning of Guidance (Habib Kathim al-Saqqaf)
- Shafi'i/Hanafi Fiqh (Shaykh Omar al-Khatib/Shaykh Amir Jameel)
- *Tawheed* (Habib Zayd)
- Forty Hadith of al-Nawawi (Shaykh Imaad)

It seems like a lot, but this year's Dowra is actually two classes shorter than last year's, so we really shouldn't be complaining about the workload.

So the day today began just like yesterday. I wish I was able to discuss the content of the classes, but unfortunately I don't have the time or the skill necessary to do so. Now that I've described what a typical day looks like, I won't be going into the minute details of the day; I'll only talk about things I didn't talk about before and any reflections/thoughts I have as they hit me. I'll try and include some interesting quotes from our teachers, and will provide translations for Arabic terms as much as I can.

---

2 The term *mawlid* is often used to describe the celebration of the birthday of the Prophet ﷺ. However, in Tarim the *mawlid* is a weekly celebration of his life.

Today I saw a little blue-eyed, blonde three-year-old girl in the mosque dressed in prayer clothes and holding her *sebah* (rosary). You know those e-mail forwards you always get showing you cute American Muslim babies? Well, in reality it's so much cuter. It got me thinking about how much environment plays a role in how you turn out to be, and what it would have been like to be raised in a place like Tarim.

Day 5 (Cont'd): The Heat

The day here is so long it almost feels like two days. Physically, we're all exhausted. The dorm where we're staying in is in one direction, Habib Umar's house in another, and Dar al-Zahra in a third. Every couple of hours we have to move around (though to be fair sometimes there is a bus to take us when it's too hot).

We're sleep deprived; we aren't used to sitting on the floor for so long; we're climbing the stairs in our dorm; we're walking around from Dar al-Zahra to our dorm to Habib Umar's house all day on rock-strewn, uneven, unpaved, uphill roads in the blistering heat dressed in black from head to toe and wearing *niqab*. I feel like I'm an old woman or that I've just come out of an intense *'umra* (lesser pilgrimage), and never have my muscles rebelled so much, not even in the most intense workout at the gym. Even my arms hurt, though I haven't been doing anything more strenuous with them than carrying my books. Probably sympathy pain!

It's also almost unbearably hot. I live in Egypt so I can't imagine what the Westerners are feeling like. Even your *eyelashes* sweat here, which means you're constantly dehydrated; I've been drinking three to four litres of water a *day*. The heat is the hardest aspect for me, even more than little sleep, since it makes me irritable and cranky. Now I wish I'd gotten one of those little fans that come free with Energizer batteries which I decided not to get so I didn't look 'stupid'.

↑ *Walking from our house to Dar al-Zahra*

But whenever I think I'm going to literally expire from the heat, I remember this quote of Habib Ali, which I read once in a brilliant testimonial by a participant about the Dowra:

"This heat is like a furnace. It will extract the imperfections of your soul, melt them away and leave you with a pure heart."

Just thinking about it immediately makes me feel better. And on the plus side, I don't think I will underestimate my air conditioner *ever* again. Or sofas and cushions. Or cold water! (The water here for washing and ablution is always hot and I assume that that's because the pipes and water tanks are outdoor. If you want cold water you have to fill up buckets with water and leave them overnight to cool.)

But it's good to endure a little difficulty - as I said before, everything we ever want is at our fingertips so how can we appreciate something if we never miss it?

Tomorrow, insha'Allah, we get to go swimming *and* attend the *mawlid*! I'm really excited about both.

Day 6: Sisterhood

We woke up today and did *du'a al-khatm* and our *wird* until sunrise. I am so glad I moved into the Dowra house, and partially because we all encourage each other: I was so tired in the morning that if it wasn't for one of my roommates telling me to get up for Fajr, I probably would have fallen back to sleep. Or I would have staggered to the bathroom, prayed, and staggered back to bed in five minutes flat.

But more than that, it's so nice to be around people 'like me', where nothing I do - like using a *siwak* (tooth-stick) for example – is strange to them. I know I come from a supposedly Arab/Muslim country, but unfortunately (and I'm generalising here), the social class I'm part of don't really have religion as a big part of their lives. In fact, being religious is something that is so 'not cool' and makes people so uncomfortable that I hesitated before beginning this diary, worrying about who was going to read it and what they would think. Then I thought to myself how ridiculous that was; I am proud my religion is so important to me, and it is nothing to hide.

So not only is everything I do normal here, but there's also peer pressure to be *good*! To attend extra sessions when we're all bone-tired, to pray in congregation etc. It's an incredible feeling that I've rarely felt in my life - peer pressure to be a better Muslim, rather than a worse one.

So back to the *du'a al-khatm* and finding it so difficult to get up. It got me thinking about how much discipline it must take to be a student here. But then I thought to myself: why is it that discipline here is much harder than discipline in anything else - back home I work all day, and then go to classes at university that can last as late at 10pm. Why can I have discipline in that area of my life but not this one? So I've decided that insha'Allah, insha'Allah I'm not going to miss any class here if I can help it, and I'm going to pray every prayer in congregation.

After our *qayloola* we went to the pool. And mash'Allah it exceeded all my expectations. As I've mentioned, the water here is always hot, so I was expecting the pool to be nothing more than a tub of hot water. But it turned out to be a *cold* pool, shaded with trees and mesh netting and surrounded by walls with windows that looked out onto a beautiful garden.

↑ *The pool...*
→ *...and the view from the windows in the pool area*

I love swimming and if I was back home now I probably would have been at the North coast swimming in the sea, so it was extra special for me. I know we've only had two days of classes, but it felt like a well-deserved holiday, and it was leisure I didn't imagine existed here. We ate crunchy apples and drank juice, and sat by the pool tanning for a bit before it got too hot. Truly, it was a highlight of the week and one that we all really enjoyed.

After we prayed Dhuhr, I made my way over to Habib Umar's house. Every day he invites over one nationality of people in Tarim to his house for lunch, and today was the day of the Egyptians. They even served us *molokheya* (traditional Egyptian soup made out of leaves. Not as weird as it sounds.)

After the Maghrib prayer in Dar al-Zahra, a girl sitting next to me introduced herself and asked what I studied at home. I told her I had studied Business at university, but then she clarified, "I meant Islamic studies," as if it was completely natural that it should be part of any school curriculum. I realised that - just like in my society I am expected to learn about balance sheets but no one thinks it's strange if I don't know how to cook or sew on a button - you're so looked down upon if you don't have a university degree but not if you've never even studied basic *fiqh* - Islamic jurisprudence.

After Maghrib was the *mawlid*. I love how ritualistic it is - they don't just read the *nasheeds* (odes) from a book, they have *bukhoor* in the entire Dar, and walked around with a bottle of *misk* for us to put on. We all got up for the *maqam*, which is a short *nasheed* praising the Prophet ﷺ, and it was beautiful. And the people are so thoughtful - after the *nasheeds* some of the students came around carrying water jugs and cups asking if anyone wanted water, knowing that our throats were probably parched from singing the *nasheeds*.

After 'Isha we came back home. Tomorrow insha'Allah is Friday and the first day of the Islamic month of Rajab, so we did *istighfar* (litanies asking for forgiveness), and some of us are now on the roof making *du'a*. I'm off to go and join them.

Day 7: Rajab

Today is the first day of Rajab, which means it's almost Sha'ban, which means it's almost Ramadan. I can't believe how quickly the year has flown by, subhan Allah. Almost everyone decided to fast today, so the *ziyaras* got cancelled and we got to sleep until 'Asr (getting up for Dhuhr, of course). We used the time to catch up on some much needed sleep and, alhamdulillah, I feel so well rested now.

The rest of the day progressed as usual: *rawha* and then class. After 'Isha we met a group who had just arrived - five from Belgium, five from Sweden and five from Denmark, who were also here for the Dowra, though they were staying in separate accommodation.

Thought: I walked alone to a class today and I was looking around when I realised - in addition to the fact that there are goats strolling around unattended - that Tarim is literally nestled within mountains, which surround it on all sides. And not mountains that are far away in the distance, but really close ones that you can walk to (at least on two sides). It's a whimsical notion, but I thought that that explained why Tarim was the way it was - as if a storm had passed over the whole world, and the mountains had protected the village, like soldiers.

Today's quote: "Doing good doesn't necessarily mean you are good, but leaving the bad means you must be." (*Habib Umar*)

After 'Isha, I picked up a book of supplications (the *Khulasa*) and I found this hadith written on the inside cover: →

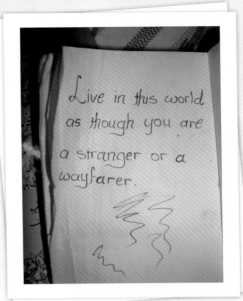

Live in this world as though you are a stranger or a wayfarer.

It sounds strange, but I feel like it was a message written to me, most probably by a previous Dowra student. When I was a child, my mum tried to explain to me the life in this world by telling me to think of a traveller crossing the desert. He stops for a little while under a tree, but ultimately has to move on. The time under the tree, of course, symbolises our time in this world. So my mother's advice is kind of the same - really good advice, though of course, very hard to implement.

Update: It turns out my mum's story comes from a hadith, and the one in the *Khulasa* was incomplete. I just read the ahadith, quoted in Imam al-Haddad's *The Lives of Man*:

"Be in the world as though a stranger or a wayfarer, and consider yourself one of the inhabitants of the graves."

and

"What have I to do with the world? The likeness of myself and the world is that of a rider travelling on a summer day, who found a tree, rested underneath it awhile, then went on, leaving it behind."

Day 8: Arabic

Today we had our first Qur'an class, and I realised I was actually really looking forward to it. It's incredible how your environment influences you. Back home my Qur'an sits for so long on my bedside table it might as well not be there. And when I do recite, it's hurriedly and without *tajweed* (rules of recitation). Here though, I found myself wanting to take a corner and *really* recite and contemplate what I was reading. I realised that I had missed the Qur'an though I wasn't aware of it. Subhan Allah.

The class also got me really thinking about Arabic. Remember the little blue-eyed American girl I mentioned a couple of entries ago? She speaks better Arabic than I do - I heard her speak to her mother in fluent *classical* Arabic.

Arabic is a sore point with me. A student from the Arabic Dowra joined us for a morning class yesterday, and asked me why I was on the English Dowra. And all the students on the English Dowra who realise that I speak Arabic have to comment on how lucky I am to be able to. But seeing them in the Qur'an class today, I felt really ashamed of myself. They all wish *so* much that they could speak and read Arabic, and here I was with it. And not only do I not appreciate the blessing, I gave it up voluntarily when I was in middle school.

I understand why non-Arab Muslims can't speak and/or read Arabic, they have a legitimate excuse. But what's my excuse for having semi-good Arabic skills? I speak Arabic fluently, but I read it not so fluently and understand classical Arabic even less. That's part of the reason I'm on an English Dowra - I probably wouldn't fare well in an all-Arabic one.

The school I was in didn't really teach us Arabic, so I used to have a Qur'an and Arabic teacher at home. But, as is the case with children, I didn't see what an amazing opportunity it was, and instead missed as many classes as I could. I eventually gave up both Arabic and Qur'an when I was around thirteen. Now I wish I had continued, instead of being stuck in this limbo state.

I'm kind of the odd one out in the Dowra; I'm literally the only non-Westerner in the group. But in life that's really how it is. I'm not a Westerner or a totally Arab citizen, and that's mainly due to the way I was raised: in completely Western schools in a completely Middle Eastern country. I'm not really stuck in the middle since both my parents are Egyptian and I was raised in Egypt but neither am I firmly on either side of the fence. Arabic is the best example I can give about my neither/nor status - it's my native tongue and yet not, if that makes sense.

But I've made it one of my resolutions here to improve my Arabic skills, even choosing to listen to the lectures of Habib Umar in Arabic, though the material is difficult enough to digest in English. I know it sounds impossible to say after such a short period of time, but I honestly feel that my Arabic is getting better and that I'm understanding more and more of the lecture each day. May Allah make it easier for me.

Today's Quote: "There are people who, like bats, see light as darkness, and are blind to the light." (*Habib Umar*)

Day 8 (Cont'd): Cleaners

The cleaners came today. Another blessing I suddenly realised I never really appreciated. Kitchen duty is hard enough (as well as handwashing my clothes in a bucket, since our washing machine is broken, which I've never done before), so I'm especially glad that they came. We were told to keep any leftovers for them, that one of them had fourteen children who eat rice "once in a blue moon", and again, I realised how blessed we are.

8

One of the things I'm never going to forget is when I was in Denmark in 2006 right after the cartoon crisis - we were invited for a *kebab* and *kofta* dinner and after we finished there was *so* much food left over, literally plates and plates of meat. I asked if we could take the food and give it to someone on the street and was told that there was no one to give the food to, and that everything was thrown away because there were no poor people. When I think of all the food that's thrown away and people going hungry in other places of the world, it's hard. One of the best charity activities I've seen in Egypt is a group of people who collect all the leftover food in hotel weddings, and distribute it to the poor.

I finally went over today to my family to have lunch and I had my favourite Tarimi meal so far: grilled chicken (better than any I've ever tasted), basmati rice, naan bread and the traditional Yemeni tomato sauce which is slightly spicy. This is the Tarimi "fast food" meal, cooked by a man in his undershirt near the one kiosk in the area.

I then went early to Dar al-Zahra today before the *rawha* and I visited the *dokan* - a little store that sells a whole lot of things. I bought a traditional Yemeni *khimar* (type of veil) - everything is sold in black plastic bags for some reason - a mulan-style fan, and some of the house dresses that women wear inside the house. The total came to just over 2,000 Yemeni riyals, which is approximately $10. I can't get over how cheap everything is here. Unfortunately, the store doesn't sell Mars ice-cream bars, which I'm really craving right now!

I also performed *wudu'* at Dar al-Zahra and it reminded me so much of *beer zamzam* in Makkah, which used to be this underground well under the area around the Kabah where you could get freezing cold *zamzam* water, named after the well it comes from. After *tawaf* (circumambulation of the Kabah) we would be so hot and literally go and shower with the cold water. Well, the water in Dar al-Zahra is freezing just like the zamzam well, and you even drink it in metal cups, just like in Makkah.

I shifted my mattress tonight directly under the fan and right in front of the air conditioner, and I truly couldn't stop smiling. I think I'm going to do a hundred alhamdulillahs every day for the blessing of the air conditioner.

Today's Quote: "If you want to be a scholar, then you will be a role model and more will be expected of you than is of other people. You must lean towards what it is the companions loved and did." (*Shaykh Omar*)

Day 9: *Humility*
Today I learnt a lesson in humility.

Yesterday I wrote an entry about Arabic and the Qur'an, how lucky I was to know Arabic, and how ashamed I was that my Arabic is so weak. But today I realised that even though I meant every word in that entry, inside I felt that I was going to be better than everyone in the house in my recitation, by virtue of the fact that Arabic is my first language and that I had learned Qur'an as a child. Kind of like the way a third grader would feel if he was put in a second grade class. He's still only a third grader, but better than a second grader.

Well, nothing put me in my place faster than spending ten minutes with my Qur'an teacher correcting the way I said the *Isti'adha* and *Bismallah* (literally *a'oodhu billahi min al-shaytan al-rajeem, bism Allahi al-rahman al-raheem*), which is how we begin reciting any surah in the Qur'an.

One of the best things about Tarim is that you know that you are definitely not the best person around. Back home, it's so easy to fall into the trap of thinking, "Oh, it's ok that I pray late, no one at work prays anyway," or "It's ok that I don't review my Qur'an, at least I've memorised some of it unlike so-and-so." Even if you don't *intend* to, you always seem to end up comparing yourself with those that seem worse off (religion-wise) than you are and coming out on top. This, in turn, keeps you resting on your laurels. Here, you feel (and know) that everyone is better than you and so you cannot fall into that trap. You'll always feel lacking, and that will insha'Allah make you better.

I forgot to mention that yesterday we began *fiqh* classes. I follow the Shafi'i *madhdhab* (school of thought), who are a minority here, so our class was held in a separate location, in Habib Umar's library. His library has fifty-six bookcases (they're numbered) with literally hundreds and hundreds of indexed books split up into topics (such as Shafi'i *fiqh*, *mawlids*, hadith explanations, etc.), mash'Allah.

I was reading *The Black Swan* right before I came to Yemen, and seeing Habib Umar's library reminded me of something the author had said in the book. He said that he knew someone who had a library with 30,000 books and that most people would admire that someone greatly and ask him how many of the books he'd read. Only a very small minority would understand something important:

"A private library is not an ego-boosting appendage but a research tool. Read books are far less valuable than unread ones. The library should contain as much of *what you do not know* as your financial means, mortgage rates, and the currently tight real-estate market will allow you to put there. You will accumulate more knowledge and more books as you grow older, and the growing number of unread books on the shelves will look at you menacingly. Indeed, the more you know, the larger the rows of unread books."[3]

---

3   Taleb, Nassim. The Black Swan: The Impact of the Highly Improbable. Random House. April 2007.

This quote reminds me of one of my favourite anonymous quotes: "What we know can fill a book. What we don't know can fill a library."

But I digress.

In the first class Shaykh Omar talked about knowledge and how to retain it. I opened the book we are studying (*Mukhtasar al-Latif*) to the first page and explained about how beginning your book with Bism Allah and alhamdulillah are so important. He told us this simple story about the importance of saying alhamdulillah about everything:

"A man was learning about Islam, and his shaykh told him how important it was to always thank Allah (say *alhamdulillah*), even for things you may think are bad for you, because you never know how something may be good for you.

One day, the man was sick. His shaykh visited him and told him to say *alhamdulillah*. The man did so.

Another time, the man got thrown in jail when he was innocent. His shaykh visited him and told him to say *alhamdulillah*. The man did so.

Another time, the man was in an accident and he lost an eye. His shaykh told him to say *alhamdulillah* but the man couldn't, telling him, "How could this be good?"

Losing all trust with the shaykh the man decided to leave his country and find a different shaykh in another one. He got on a ship, and the ship sank. The people on board grabbed planks and drifted until they reached an island.

It turned out the island was inhabited by carnivores, whose custom was to eat anyone whole and healthy. But because of the man's eye, they let him live."

So it's a small story, but I thought it really illustrated how we never know what might be good for us and where our benefit lies.

Today in class, Shaykh Omar asked a question and wondered out loud if any of the women would like to answer. Until now, he is the only teacher who has actively acknowledged us, and it made me so happy I answered straight way. Alhamdulillah my answer was correct. (Four ways to retain knowledge: review with others, teach others, repeat what you've studied over and over, and write it down.)

Yesterday was also the anniversary of the Rihla. I realised that in terms of classes, the Rihla was definitely more intensive, or at least I felt that we covered a lot more material. And because the classes in Habib Umar's house are not translated simultaneously, lesson time is automatically cut in half.

However, I feel that I'm learning more from this experience than in the Rihla. As strange as it sounds, Tarim seems to be more spiritual than Saudi Arabia; I feel that here religion is really reflected within the people and that they really have faith, and not just the outward manifestations of religion. That influences us in ways we might not even feel. Personally, I feel that I'm getting more out of the place and the people than the classes, which is more than enough for me. Just being here I do things that I find so hard to do back home, and what's more, I wonder why on earth was it hard?

Today we ate Tarimi bread, *heef*, which looks like roti, and it was really good. We also had spaghetti for dinner, and you could just see the joy on everyone's faces. We definitely eat enough here, but the menu is always more or less the same: curry and rice.

Today I also bought the edition of the book we are studying in the *rawha* printed specially for this Dowra, *Mannerisms of the Self* by Imam Abd-Allah al-Bosayry and alhamdulillah it makes the *rawha* so much easier to follow. It wasn't included in our packet because it's only available in Arabic, and hopefully it can also help me improve my Arabic.

Today's Quote: "Guard your tongue. A scholar once said, when asked why he didn't speak often: 'I have two ears and one tongue. And that tongue is guarded by two sets of barriers: the teeth and the lips.' Backbiting is worse than thirty-six acts of fornication. You see how Islam protects the reputation of the Muslim? You are backbiting even if you think the thoughts in your heart and don't say them out loud." (*Habib Kathim*)

A chilling thought. That you are not only judged for vocal backbiting, one of the sins of the tongue which, according to the Qur'an, is equivalent to eating the flesh of your dead brother, but for backbiting him (or her) in your mind:

"O you who believe! Avoid most of suspicion, for surely suspicion in some cases is a sin, and do not spy nor let some of you backbite others. Does one of you like to eat the flesh of his dead brother? But you abhor it; and be careful of (your duty to) Allah, surely Allah is Oft-returning (to mercy), Merciful." (Surat al-Hujurat 49:12)

Day 10: Qur'an Class

I had my second Qur'an class today. Subhan Allah we all made so many mistakes while reciting the *Fatiha* (the first surah of the Qur'an) which Muslims recite a minimum of seventeen times a day while praying. Especially with the Bism Allah. We all pronounce it "*Bism Allah*" when actually it's "*Bi'ism Allah*". I tried to console myself by telling myself that at least my mistakes were ones we all made, but I wasn't really all that successful. And it turns out I'm not really good at reciting in front of many people; I get really nervous.

And I just felt worse when the teacher – who, coincidentally, *also* happens to be Egyptian - advised us to get a Qur'an teacher when we get back home and some of the students said they wouldn't be able to find one. I thought of the numerous teachers I had had as a child and never appreciated. And how, as we say in Arabic:

التعلم في الصغر كالنقش على الحجر , والتعلم في الكبر كالنقش على الماء

"Learning when you're young is like carving into a rock and learning when you're old is like carving into water."

My teacher thinks I should memorise *Surat al-Kahf* (The Cave) while I'm here. I was thinking of *Surah Yaseen* since it's half the length of *Al-Kahf*, but *Al-Kahf* it is. That's 110 verses in eleven and a half pages, which is an average of almost three pages a week. It sounds better when I say five verses a day but still I don't think I'll be able to do it. But insha'Allah I aim to have at least half of it memorised.

Today's Quote: "All Muslims know three ahadith: 'Acts are by intentions', '*Istafti qalbak* [Ask your heart]', and 'Religion is [making things] easy', which they use to justify their actions. They do bad deeds but say their intention is good. They make their own decision regarding questions they have, not realising that you should only 'ask your heart' if you find that scholars are equally divided over the issue. They ignore things they should do because they say they're too hard." (*Shaykh Imaad*)

Day 10 (Cont'd): The People of Tarim

Today we drove up one of the mountains that surround Tarim. A nerve-wracking, teeth-grinding ten minutes in our bus and we reached Habib Umar's home in the mountains. I still have no idea how the bus tyres don't puncture on the sharp rocks. You know how goats can clamber up mountains? Well, our bus clambers up roads like a goat clambers up a mountain.

The view at the house is incredible. From there, you can see all of Tarim, and I was right - it literally is nestled between awe-inspiring mountains. Some of them have names of Allah written on rocks in white chalk that you can see from far away. It was so dark I didn't even notice the mountains at first and was thinking, "Why does this horizon look so strange?" for a good bit before I realised they were mountains.

→ *Allah is written in white chalk on the mountain*

I walked around the house with two Yemeni girls (the girls of Dar al-Zahra were also invited) and one of my housemates and I ended up sitting on the ledge of the mountain with them. There was a wedding going on nearby and it sounded exactly like the *zaffa* (wedding procession) in Egypt; I saw a car earlier that day decorated with "*Mabrouk*" (congratulations, the equivalent of "Just Married") and I assume it was probably for the same wedding. Anyway, we sat on the ledge and the girls asked Eva (who is from Bulgaria) to tell them the story of her conversion to Islam.

No matter how many converts I listen to or how mundane they think their stories are, I will always remain in awe of them. Just remembering Eva talking about how her parents didn't even show up to her wedding or how she decided to put on the *hijab* in her workplace rather than applying for a new job because she saw it as Allah's test for her gives me goosebumps. And it makes my own problems seem petty and insignificant.

Every day, I am just bowled over by the kindness of the people here. Ustadha Moneeba, our house *mushrifa* (supervisor) is one of the kindest women I have *ever* met. I forgot my books on the mountain and when I called her to tell her she made the bus she was on turn around to go back and get them, though it was the middle of the night and she must have been dead tired. I will never forget how she greeted me the first day I met her in Dar al-Zahra when my family's neighbour took me over; she greeted me like a long lost sister, with hugs and kisses, and none of it was faking - she was genuinely happy to meet me.

She keeps telling us how *khidma* (service) is one of the most important things we could be doing. Prophet Muhammad ﷺ used to serve others, exemplifying a substantial principle of Islamic leadership: the master of the people is the one who serves them. Ustadha Moneeba is the embodiment of her advice to us. She never asks anyone for *anything*, and is instead always doing things for us herself, making us really ashamed of not helping around the house more. And she's not just any volunteer: she's a teacher with years of experience.

She's on the go twenty-four/seven, rarely sleeps because she's organising stuff for us, and is always *always* cheerful. I've always hated constantly perky people, but for some reason I don't feel the same way about her. Perhaps because I feel that she's not only sincere but that for her, helping us truly stems from a love of us for the sake of Allah.

Khidma is something everyone here strives to do; I just learned today that our bus driver - who comes over twice every prayer to take us to class and waits outside for us in an un-air-conditioned microbus in the boiling sun - is not a bus driver, but a student at Dar al-Mustafa engaged in *da'wah* who is doing this for us voluntarily.

People here are *so* nice you think they *must* be faking, only there's something about them that tells you they're not. Their kindness puts me at a loss for words, unbelieving that they truly could have no 'barriers' put up at all, that they lay themselves bare in front of you. It forces you to reciprocate and to, in turn, lower your guard.

Neighbours treat you better than family relatives do. The neighbours of my family here in Tarim have been so, so, so, so kind it's unbelievable. Back home, I know the names of my neighbours and I smile at them when I see them in the elevator, and that's about it. And they've been our neighbours for almost a dozen years.

My family's neighbours in Tarim, an elderly couple, have been their neighbours for one week and their kindness puts us to shame. The man took my brother around the city (and he's a diabetic with a knee problem), introduced him to all the shaykhs, and walks to the market every day in the morning to buy my family fruit and fish though they beg him not to.

The woman has blood pressure problems and can't walk far and yet insists on walking my mother to Dar al-Zahra so she doesn't walk alone, lending her an iron, sending food upstairs, inviting my family for dinner *every* night, and basically everything she can think of. I spent one night with my family this week and when she found out she insisted she fry me some chips. And when I said no she still made them anyway, got her husband to walk to the *dokan* at night to buy me bread, and walked up three flights of stairs to give them to me. Honestly, they are so kind I don't know what to make of them. I have never *ever* met anyone like them in my life.

When I think of the companions of the Prophet Muhammad ﷺ saying that the Prophet advised them about neighbours so much they thought he would tell them to include neighbours in their wills, I now only think of this couple. They *truly* implement the Prophet's teachings more than anyone I have *ever* met in my life, for absolutely no benefit.

There must be bad people in Tarim, it's not paradise and I'm not naive enough to think there aren't any. But here, you feel that the inherent goodness in people, the *fitra* (primordial nature), is truly present, and not buried like it is with so many of us in this day and age. And it's a goodness that I'm sure needs no religion - an atheist could come here and still be moved by these people, who truly embody the spirit of *al-Ethar* so much more than I could ever dream of being. Al-Ethar is a verb that comes from the Qur'an, and the closest translation is altruism. It is more than that, however. It has three meanings: giving away what you have to others, even if you need it, *and* you are happy about it.

There's a hadith that says:
"None of you truly believes until he loves for his brother what he loves for himself." (*Al-Bukhari*)

That is, your *iman* (faith) is not complete until you truly wish that every good thing that happens to you also happens to other people. If you think about it, it's near impossible to do. But here, you feel that people truly wish only great things for you.

Today's Quote: "Knowledge won't help you unless you implement it, just like water won't help a thirsty person until he drinks it." (*Habib Umar*)

Day 11: Girl Talk

I've just come out of an intense and raw 'sharing our feelings' session.

I've never been a sharing person. Or a girly-touchy-huggy-feely person. I find it very hard to express my feelings face to face, and I've always been the person rolling my eyes at people crying and going, "What on earth are they crying about?" But this session was different somehow. It was different because we weren't talking about our friendships or our problems in life, but about our relationship with God. It was private and emotional and almost fragile to talk about - you know the butterfly emerging from a cocoon? It has to struggle for exactly the right amount of time or else its wings won't be strong enough to carry it. That's how I feel talking about today's session, like I'm walking on eggshells. I either do it right or else I fail completely and make something that was so special seem so awkward and stilted.

I can't believe how open everyone was and how willing they were to put themselves 'out there', and I'm sure part of it is because they were influenced by the genuineness of the people we've met, who literally stump you with their sincerity. In real life, you would never share so much of yourself with anyone who wasn't a true life-long friend, let alone people you've known for a week. Partly because of the fact that it's simply 'not done', but largely because of self-preservation. Because to make yourself vulnerable and voice your fears out loud takes tremendous courage, to entrust your feelings to another person who may cradle them just as easily as trample all over them.

It's even more difficult when it comes to religion, which is such a taboo, controversial and loaded topic that people have chosen to ignore it completely. The moment you start speaking about religion you can almost see peoples' eyes shutter and they look away, desperately trying to find a way to extricate themselves from an uncomfortable situation.

We were asked to state our intention for the rest of the Dowra and why we came. And subhan Allah, it wasn't until I began formulating my thoughts and articulating them that I fully realised what I was feeling. And in honour of the girls who were so much braver and honest than I was in detailing their perceived faults, I'm going to share something with the world:

Sometimes, I look around at everyone with me in this house and think, "What on earth am I doing here?" I feel that I'm acting out a role - that deep down I'm not really at all spiritual or religious. I know what *iman* is and I can see it in people, but I just feel that I haven't tasted it myself. I feel that the outward manifestations of religion - like praying and fasting and *hijab* - are the only religious aspects about me. I see people crying when they listen to a certain story about the Prophet ﷺ or Allah and I wonder why I'm not as moved as they are, and why my heart seems to have hardened over the years.

I definitely know that I want to *be* one of these people and that's part of the reason I'm here - I keep hoping that some magic wand will pass over me and turn me into one of those serene people who seem to 'glow' with inner light. But unfortunately, so far I'm still the same old me, surrounded by all these incredible people.

But then I think to myself that at least while I'm in the midst of these people, I might absorb some of their goodness by osmosis. And if not, then perhaps I might be 'swept away' in the middle of them, that even though my heart may not be actively engaged in *dhikr* or making *du'a* these actions may be accepted by virtue of the people around me. I think of the hadith where Allah tells His angels to forgive the sins of everyone sitting remembering Him, even the person who was there for a completely different reason or didn't want to be there; that He'll forgive him too, simply because he was in the presence of those who were truly good at heart.

So I'm that person on the fringes, who wants to get in with the good people though he himself isn't one of them. I love those great people and aspire to be like them and believe in the hadith that says:

"A person will be with whom he loves [on judgement day]." (*Al-Bukhari*)

So I'll just hang on to their coattails and hope for the best.

We were told today that Tarim exposes you. Not just to others but to yourself. And it's true. Every passing day I am more and more disgusted with myself. I see how the people here lead their lives, wasting not a single moment and how I waste months and months with vapid, useless things. Things I think I can't live without, but that I haven't missed at all since I've been here. To us, people whose work and activities define who we are, the people's lives here seem empty. And yet, they are fuller than we could ever aspire to have our lives be.

So why did I come here? To be honest, the biggest reason was self-reflection, maybe even more than knowledge; to separate and dissociate myself from all the mundane, time-consuming and trivial aspects of my life that eat away so much of my time; to focus on the reason I was created; to take a time-out of my busy, busy life and see where I want to go from here; to figure out if the path I'm on and what I'm doing with my life, is the best I could be doing; to figure out why I feel that with every passing day my faith is getting weaker and that spiritually I've never been lower though nothing has changed in my behaviour; to 'collect' as much *hasanat* (good deeds) as I could; to analyse the shortcomings in my character and how to change what I can; to improve my Arabic; to figure out my intentions in my actions and why they are so mixed; to meet people like myself; to meet people so much better than I am and to realise what a long way I have to go; to *itbahdil shiwaya* (roughing it) to strengthen my character.

At the end of the session, we were told to reflect on the fact that we were chosen not only to come here, but to come here with the people living with us in the house. That we were going to get a chance to experience a unique bond of sisterhood, loving each other purely for the sake of Allah. And although something in me groaned a little bit at the clichéd-ness of it all, another part of me smiled wistfully.

Today's quote: "The experience here makes me feel like the seven dwarves rolled into one. The heat makes me like grumpy and sleepy especially. I feel that you got stuck with me here, and that you're all so much better than I am. I'm scared to go back home and not have this aura of spirituality that everyone who comes here has when they go back to their homes, and to have people ask, 'Wait, wasn't she in Tarim?' (*My roommate Choclit, who was the bravest one of us all*)

Day 12: Zambal

Today we visited Zambal, the special graveyard reserved for the *awliya'* of Tarim (patron saints is the closest definition - descendants of the Prophet Muhammad ﷺ). It is said that forty *sahaba* (Companions of the Prophet ﷺ) from the Battle of Badr are buried in the Zambal Cemetary along with seventy other *sahaba*. All other Tarimis are buried in Bashshar, the normal cemetery.

Muslim graveyards are usually simply an enclosed area with no headstones, so it was initially strange to see hundreds of them. And not neat, straight-in-a-line headstones on even ground, but ones arranged in no particular order in an extremely small area. We went at night and it was utterly silent. If you visualise it, it must look like a scene from a horror movie. But even a passing cat with an arched back didn't seem at all spooky. On the contrary, it was extremely, extremely peaceful. Serene even. I felt like I could spend the night there and not be at all freaked out. More than one person commented on how different the atmosphere was to ones in normal graveyards.

↑ *Zambal Cemetery at night*

Habib Umar's wife came with us and led us in making *du'a*. We stood in front of *al-Faqih al-Muqadam's* grave, who was an incredible scholar and pious man. It was definitely an experience. But I'm not exactly sure what I feel. Like I was saying yesterday, I looked around me at the people crying and felt like a dunce in a class, frustrated because I'm not able to reach that spiritual 'high'. Part of me was saying, "It's a graveyard." But another part was definitely moved and awed, recognising that there were great people buried where I was standing.

It also rained today. I have no idea how rain could possibly come down in this heat, but it did. And lightning too.

Day 13: Relax

It's the weekend again and a full week of classes has passed. I've gotten used to sitting on the floor and my muscles aren't protesting like they did in the first week. I'm also really getting used to the schedule, so much that I woke up today at 9am and literally had to force myself to go back to sleep.

I've always been the kind of person who when they wake up stay up no matter how little sleep they got, alhamdulillah I haven't been finding it hard to stay awake in classes. Whenever I find my concentration wavering though, I remind myself about how many pointless books and movies I've watched and wasted time doing so - and tell myself I can definitely stay focused for one more hour.

But I can't help thinking that it must be a punishing schedule if you live here. Today we have nothing until the *rawha* at 4pm and although that's how I usually spend my weekends at home (sometimes I literally do nothing the whole day), I feel strange having so much free time.

And that got me thinking: am I being so diligent in waking up for Tahajjud and attending every class because I know it's for a limited amount of time and not forever? Would I be so attentive if I was a student at Dar al-Zahra? Or if I lived here? It's a difficult question and I'm not sure if my answer right now would be yes.

There's an optional session right now by Habib Umar's wife about raising your children in the West and I opted to skip it (since it wasn't really relevant to me) in order to start memorising *Surat al-Kahf* and have some time to think when the house wasn't full of women. Thank goodness the electricity was back on - yesterday the generator kept dying and all of us were sitting around, unwilling to move, *mifalfaseen* (an Arabic expression for when a fish is out of the water and jumps around for a bit before giving up).

So I was sitting in the atypical silence thinking and I realised that I was looking at the clock every ten minutes. Shaykh Hamza Yusuf was so correct to say that many of us have lost the ability to be silent and that meditating, or even some light reflection, is becoming impossible. There's a study out right now that says when asked to sit in a room and meditate, most Americans had an anxiety attack. We simply can't be doing *nothing* anymore; we can't be content with our own thoughts to entertain us. Shaykh Hamza called our generation the iPod generation and nothing could be closer to the truth. Substitute the iPod for anything - music, books, movies, talking on the phone, Facebook, etc. and that's who we are.

So I left the clock behind and I climbed upstairs to the roof. And truly, it was like I had left this realm for another one, as new-agey as that sounds. Silence is defined as the utter absence of sound. We do get silence in Egypt, though very rarely. But it's a different kind of silence - even without noise you feel that the air *thrums* with vibrancy; the atmosphere itself is not still. Here, stillness permeates the air which has no zing to it, I could literally feel my heart rate slowing down to match it. The view of the mountains surrounding me on all sides and the hot air blowing like a hairdryer in my face literally changed my *hal* (state). My voice on the wind reciting Qur'an felt unnatural, almost as if it was causing ripples in the air. That's how still it was. It gave me goosebumps and I automatically lowered my voice.

↓ *View from the rooftop of the Dowra house*

And yet, it was an incredible experience. I will definitely be doing my memorisation on the roof from now on, insha'Allah.

Today's Quote: "Your *hal* when you pray is a mirror of your relationship with Allah." (*Habib Umar*)

Another (later) quote: "[And] your *hal* on hearing the *adhan* reflects what your *hal* will be on leaving this world. Are you yearning to hear it?" (*Habib Umar*)

Day 13 (Cont'd): Shaykh Abu Bakr bin Salem

Remember a few days ago I was talking about the hospitality of people in Tarim? Well, today I have another example of how incredible it is.

↓ *A traditional Yemeni meal*

My family was telling our neighbour how they hadn't yet tasted Yemeni food and so she got *her* friend to cook us a traditional Yemeni meal: rice cooked in a special clay oven called a *meefa* which cooks food over coal; meat that takes four hours to cook; *qurooba*, a special kind of potato; and *roya*, a salad made out of pineapple, apple, and cucumber with *tamr hindy* (tamarind) sauce. And all of it served with the traditional Yemeni red tomato sauce which turns out to be called *beesbas*. And the woman had never even met us.

What's more, we told her we hadn't yet gone to visit any of the major Tarimi landmarks and she gets her husband to take us. She doesn't know us, may have had something else planned that day and yet she dropped everything for us. She asked us where we wanted to go and we said to visit the grave of Shaykh Abu Bakr bin Salem, who was a great scholar who lived approximately four hundred years ago. He was said to be so pious he didn't speak a word to anyone for forty years, instead spending his time worshipping Allah. It's said he used to walk from 'Inat - where he lived and his gravesite is located - to Tarim every day. 'Inat is approximately twenty minutes out of Tarim by *car*. Shaykh Abu Bakr's *wird* is one of the most famous ones there are being used to this very day.

And not only did the couple take us, but her husband acted as a tour guide explaining everything on the way to us. The view on our way there was gorgeous. It was a bit cramped in the car so I decided to sit in the trunk, but that way I got an even better view from out of the back window. I know I saw the view on my way to Tarim, but I was so tired from travelling I wasn't really concentrating. It's a disconcerting thing to look out on one side and see humungous mountains and desert versus dozens and dozens of palm trees and lush foliage on the other.

→ *Valley of palm trees outside Tarim on the way to 'Inat*

But I guess it makes sense when you realise that Tarim is essentially a giant system of *wadis* (valleys) that are irrigated by rainfalls. It's incredible to realise that now it is so, so hot but then in the rainy season it rains so much you can't travel to Seiyun because the roads are flooded. It's even stranger to think that one day, a long, long time ago, all of Tarim was under the sea.

So we visited the grave of the shaykh and his sons, and again, just like Zambal, the graveyard was very peaceful. It was so quiet I could hear birds chirping - and for all we know they may have been doing their own *dhikr*.

↓ *Cemetery*
↘ *where Shaykh Abu Bakr bin Salem is buried*

↓ *Sun setting in the cemetery*

The couple could have then thought, "We've done enough," but no, they also took us to the shaykh's house, which is located in what looks like an alleyway straight out of Aladdin. The house is

only one room and one bathroom and has stood there for hundreds of years. The bed frame is still there and each corner has a place where *misk* would be placed. I'm guessing someone has continued in the tradition, because it still smelled like incense.

↑ *Shaykh Abu Bakr bin Salem's house*

The couple then took us home in time for the *mawlid* and promised that insha'Allah they would show us all the landmarks in Tarim whenever we had the time. And these were people we had just met. Subhan Allah.

I also learnt today that people here get married very young. I knew they did - I read about a study conducted by Yemen's Women and Development Study Centre in June 2008 that says that over half of women who marry in Yemen are under fifteen, but it didn't really register for some reason. I asked the Yemeni woman with us today how old she was and she said in her early thirties. But, she added, she got married at fifteen, and so did her daughter, who got engaged at eleven to a man she never saw until her wedding night.

It seems so strange and alien to me. I'm twenty-one, and yet to her second daughter, who asked me how old I was, I was a spinster, "My cousin is twenty-one with five children," she told me. (And can I just add it's bad enough to get the spinster spiel from my grandma, let alone from a fourteen-year-old?) To them, early marriage is a way of life and I guess with the extremely segregated society it makes some sense to me.

But I can't imagine that at fifteen I could have been married. I can hardly envision being married now and taking care of a house, husband and children. Part of it, I'm sure, is that it takes us a lot longer to mature now. A twenty-year-old today is not like a twenty-year-old half a century ago.

Day 13 (Cont'd): Tarimi Culture

Other random things I've learnt about Tarimi/Yemeni culture so far:

- The preferred method of transportation is by motorcycle.
- Yemeni *nasheeds* are beautiful.
- Men wear wrap around skirts that kind of look like sarongs only they're not rucked up at one side of course. Many also wear *kohl* (eyeliner). Many also walk around barefoot on the rocky streets.
- There are women who work in the fields in full *niqab*. They wear tall 'witch' hats or sombrero looking ones made out of straw to protect themselves from the sun and often herd goats.
- Almost everyone sits on the floor here - in class, to eat, to talk, and even to sleep.
- At home, women wear extremely colourful house dresses which resemble *jalabiyas*. I bought and wore my first one a couple of days ago.
- Yemeni honey makes any bread taste like *feteer meshaltet* (a type of sweet pastry that looks like a really big, thick pancake).
- When they pray, women wear a *kamees*, which ties around their head (it's usually colourful). They then put the *siwak* in the tie around their head. And most then wear a *hijab* over the *kamees*. There's also a loop at the wrist to place over the thumb so the sleeves don't fall back to show your forearms.
- People here do have fun - I saw a football field today and men in football uniforms.
- The *Fatiha* is a way of life here. After everything and anything they do, everyone must recite the *Fatiha*.

← *Woman herding
goats outside Tarim*

→ *Goats in Tarim*

↑ *Men at the cemetery*

→ *Little girl visiting the grave of Shaykh Abu Bakr bin Salem with her family*

Day 14: The Graves of Tarim

Today we visited more graves in Tarim. One of my housemates has a book titled *The Graves of Tarim* by Engseng Ho and I envied her for her preparedness, mash'Allah. But who would have thought there'd be a book specifically for the graves in Tarim?

First, we visited the grave of Imam al-Muhajir (the migrant) Ahmed bin 'Isa, from whom all of the *sayyids* of Hadhramaut are descended (the Ba 'Alawis/Banu 'Alawis). They're called the 'Alawis after the muhajir's grandson, who became the ancestor of all 'Alawi *sayyids*.

Al-Muhajir was a very rich man in Iraq who left everything behind and migrated to many countries and cities before ultimately ending up in al-Husaya, a place between Seiyun and Tarim. He is called "the migrant for the sake of Allah" because he moved wanting to find a place where his children could grow up properly. He died in 965 CE and his grave is located under a white dome up the side of a *wadi*, at the top of a very long flight of steps carved into the rock (193 steps, to be exact! I counted). Although the steps were shallow, I couldn't believe how unfit we all were. Someone had put a tank of cool water at the top for people to drink from and I couldn't help thinking what a wonderful *sadaqah jariya* (ongoing charity) that must be.

← *The grave of Ahmed bin 'Isa, Al-Muhajir*

→ *At the top of the staircase of Al-Muhajir's mausoleum*

On our way down, we also passed to give our salams to the maternal great-grandfather of Imam al-Haddad, Sayyid Ahmad al-Habashi, who was buried at the bottom of the staircase.

↓ *Sign at the tomb of Sayyid Ahmad al-Habashi*

↑ *View back down from the top of Al-Muhajir's staircase*

We then visited Shaykha Sultana, who was an incredible woman. It is said that she was from *Ahl al-Khata* (The People of the Steps), who could move great distances, so she would go to Makkah every day to do *'umra*. She could see the Prophet Muhammad ﷺ whenever she wanted. She was such a pious woman that when Abd al-Rahman al-Saqqaf - who was a great scholar of his time - asked for her hand in marriage, she declined, telling him not in this world but in the next, because he was a descendent of the Prophet and she didn't want to taint his children's lineage because she wasn't.

→ *Dome at the mausoleum of Shakykha Sultana*

↓ *Old Qur'ans inside the mausoleum of Shaykha Sultana*

Seeing the incredible reverence people here have for visiting graves makes me think of how little we have for the great people buried in Egypt: Imam al-Shafi'i, al-Husayn the grandson of the Prophet Muhammad ﷺ, Nafeesat al-'Ilm, the granddaughter of al-Husayn, and many many more.

And of course, it makes me reflect on all the times I've visited the Prophet's grave in his mosque in Madinah and simply been content with a quick salam. Now I know better.

Today's quote: "**Prophet Nuh** ﷺ was walking one day when he came across a mutated dog. He commented, 'What an ugly dog.' God gave the dog the ability to speak and it said, 'If it was up to me, I wouldn't have created myself like this, but this is how Allah made me. Are you blaming the creation or the creator?' And Prophet Nuh ﷺ cried so much that's how he got his name - *nuh* comes from *niyah*, which means uncontrollable tears. So never curse anything Allah has created." (*Habib Kathim*)

Another one of the many, many sins of the tongue. Imam al-Ghazali has mentioned eighteen, but the eight main ones are: lying, breaking promises, backbiting, argumentation, praising yourself, cursing, invoking evil on people/things, and mockery.

Day 14 (Cont'd): Habib Ali

Habib Ali finally arrived today and we had our very first class with him after 'Isha.

Being here in Tarim and having such limited access to the shaykhs because I'm a woman has made me realise how lucky I was to have had such access to them in my normal life. The first time I really met Habib Ali was in Abu Dhabi in a small private setting where I had the chance to sit with him and ask him questions face to face. It's embarrassing to admit, but my only question to him then was whether or not I could have highlights in my hair. Ok, so it's stupid and a complete waste of an opportunity but I was only fifteen at the time.

But it's *because* Habib Ali didn't just tell me, "What a stupid question to ask," and sat with me and spent half an hour of his time answering me that I decided this wasn't a shaykh just like every other one. True, he *looked* like every other shaykh I had disliked growing up - the turban-clad heavily bearded men who only spewed vitriol about the hell-fire and the heedlessness of today's youth, but he was very different.

"The first thing you notice about Habib Ali is his smile," begins an incredible article written about him in 2006 by the UK based magazine Q-News. That article was a large reason why I decided to become a journalist.

And it's so true. Habib Ali is a person who truly makes you feel that religion is not this humungous burden on our shoulders that we have to carry balanced on a plank over quicksand, but an honour that has been bestowed upon us. I always leave his lectures - which are always riveting and easy to follow - invigorated and optimistic. He has a certain aura around him and charisma that makes people want to listen to him. He is always so sincere and so enthusiastic about his mission - anyone else would have buckled under the huge responsibility he has undertaken.

Like all the *habayeb*, Habib Ali is:
"Firmly Sunni, Husayni in lineage, Shafi'i in *fiqh*, Ash'ari in *aqida* (creed) and Ghazalian in behaviour." *(Quote is from a brother's wonderful account of his time in Tarim)*

Habib Ali's lectures revolve around *da'wah* and again, I realised how lucky I was to be here. I mean, all these Westerners are the ones who will benefit most from this Dowra, since they go back to their countries and actively implement all these teachings. Sometimes I wonder if I took the place of someone who was more deserving to be here, since in the end I'm just an Egyptian who will go back home to Egypt. At the same time I think, well, you never know where your path may lead.

Today's Quote: "Speak to people in the language of the smile." (*Habib Ali*)

Day 15: Tired

I'm feeling very out of sorts today. I have a splitting headache, I'm really tired, and I've skipped a couple of meals trying to get some sleep so I'm also really hungry.

Being tired, drained and hungry is no fun. It makes me cranky and everything seems to get on my nerves, from the Qur'an class this morning which lasted forty-five minutes longer than it should have, to trying to sleep and all five girls in the room deciding that now was the time to talk. I'm not feeling very sunshiny today.

My roommate has a theory that everyone who comes back from the Dowra seems changed because in these forty days they break their *nafs* - they have to endure the heat, the lack of sleep, the restricted menu options, showering in a bucket etc., and so they come back changed. (The *nafs* is the Islamic concept of the self - an entity separate from the soul which craves all the worldly desires. Your *nafs* is usually what you refer to when you say "I want," rather than your soul, which has different needs that people usually ignore.)

In *Agenda to Change our Condition*, we're told that to discipline the *nafs* one needs to "eat less, talk less, sleep less." I know that and I know that I'm putting myself through these difficulties for a reason. But right now, all I want is a zinger sandwich from KFC, fries from McDonalds, an ice-cold Pepsi and a Cadbury Dairy Milk bar. While watching *Kutch Kutch Hota Hai*. Or the new Will Smith movie (Han something?).

Today's Quote: "You can't just come to Tarim, and expect the Aunties who clean the house to take your *nafs* and wash and polish it for you. You have to work at it yourself." (*Ustadha Moneeba, our house supervisor*)

There goes my little wish bubble. No magic wand here.

Day 15 (Cont'd): Food

We just had lunch and I'm feeling a lot better. True, it was the same rice and curry mix we have almost every day, but I guess I was hungrier than I realised because eating made me feel better. Plus we got some chocolate milk and I feel as though the much-needed chocolate went straight to my head. But just in case I came across as an unusually uptight person when it comes to food, let me explain myself. The food here doesn't really vary:

> **Breakfast:** Bread with triangle cheese spreads (*La vache que rit* wannabes) and beans/eggs
> **Lunch:** Rice and curry
> **Dinner:** Soup and bread

It's also usually unseasoned - I find myself putting anything I can find on the rice to give it flavour: vinegar, ketchup, yogurt, and even an orange once. But it is definitely more than enough and we do have a lot of little luxuries - fizzy drinks (you should have seen the expressions on everyone's faces when they were delivered) and chocolate spread especially. And we're lucky - the variety of food this year, according to one of my housemates who was here two years ago, has more than doubled.

But here you do realise how spoiled we've become when it comes to food. Back home, I'm at work most of the day and then I have classes in the evening and so I eat out a lot of the time. Or I simply pick up the phone and order whatever I feel like that day - shanghai wings from Chilis, butter chicken from Maharaja, beef barbeque from Peking, a bagel, a pizza, a *shawerma* sandwich etc.

Plus, you realise how attached we've become to desserts, the one thing that we *definitely* don't have easy access to here. Chocolates, candy, cakes, ice-cream etc.; things that we get just by standing at any checkout till in any supermarket, are as rare as rain is here.

And even if you do get access to candy here (or even normal food like tuna or cornflakes) - by getting the husband/brother of one of the women to buy it since women aren't allowed in stores here - you feel guilty about hoarding it and eating it like a fugitive in your room because you want to offer some to the rest of your housemates but know that you don't have enough to go around. As Muslims, one of the only *halal* (divinely permissible) pleasures available to us at a certain stage in our life is food. But sometimes, we forget that gluttony is also a sin - Prophet Muhammad ﷺ said you should never feel full, and that a third of your stomach should always be empty. How many of us actually implement that advice?

Nor do we realise what a blessing it is to have such an incredible variety of foods - the Prophet and his companions were once going to battle and they had only dates to sustain them; they would place a date on their tongues until it dissolved. The Prophet ﷺ told them that there would come a day when they would have *two* types of food in one meal. They were astonished and unbelieving. Now, how many types of food do we eat in a day?

So what I guess I'm trying to say is that the lack of variety of food in this Dowra is a hidden blessing. Diet potential aside (joke!), we will be able to appreciate food back home a lot more than we do, plus we have the opportunity to reel in our *nafs* which we may have been giving free reign to with regards to food.

And something else to remember. Imam al-Ghazali said: "There is no vessel more hateful to God than a stomach full of lawful food. [...] Satiety hardens the heart."

Day 16: Reflections on Classes

Qur'an: Alhamdulillah, the class is going well. We're studying *tajweed* and memorising verses and reciting them. I've set aside forty-five minutes a day for memorisation.

Fiqh: This is probably one of my favourite classes. Shaykh Omar is an incredibly good teacher. He cracks jokes, he's humorous, he asks the women questions (and gives us a thumbs up on our TV screen when we get the correct answer), he gives us anecdotes so we can really understand what he's explaining, and he is very thorough in his explanations. Although I've already studied much of what he's explaining (for example, how to perform *wudu'*), it's a really good refresher course and I'm still learning a lot of things I didn't know.

Al-Rawha: This is the most difficult class we are studying, though probably one of the most important. Basically, we are studying a book called *Mannerisms of the Self* and a *qaseeda* (poem) by Imam al-Haddad titled, "If you want to live happily for the duration of your life [you should]...". The *qaseeda* then gives us advice about living our lives, things like reciting the Qur'an and sticking to our prayers.

How the class works is that the *qaseeda* is first recited. Then random men in the audience are chosen by Habib Umar to read a couple of pages each from the book (usually around ten pages a day). The book isn't easy - I think it's the only book other than the Qur'an that I've seen with all the *nahw* (Arabic grammar) printed in it - and so Habib Umar corrects the men often. Then Habib Umar begins by explaining a couple of verses from the *qaseeda* before beginning to explain the topic addressed in the book. The topics are all related to the discipline of the self (*nafs*): its diseases and how to deal with them.

The topics addressed in the *rawha* are probably some of the most abstract ones we deal with, because they're not issues you can really concretely deal with, like knowing how to pray. Ok, so I learn to recognise when I'm suffering from pride, but how do I change myself? How do I make myself truly love for my brother what I want for myself? One of my roommates was saying how hard it is to realise that you have all these weaknesses in character and to not be able to fix them easily. It's frustrating, she said, because we all know that we have to take it one step at a time, but it's like telling yourself you have to take out one piece of trash at a time from a landfill.

The *rawha* is also quite intense and needs a lot of concentration, especially since Habib Umar speaks in very classical Arabic. I've listened to it at home on the radio twice and I realised that I concentrate better there than at Dar al-Zahra, where there's the distraction of people and the TV screen. Plus, I then have approximately an hour between the time the *rawha* ends and Maghrib prayer to study, time which is usually wasted at Dar al-Zahra because an hour is too short to go home but there's not much studying we can do there.

Nevertheless, I've decided to attend the *rawha* at Dar al-Zahra as often as I can because in the end, sitting at home in my house dress is not a *majlis 'ilm* (study setting). There are no angels attending and I don't get the *'ajr* (reward) I would if I got up, got dressed, and walked in the heat to attend. Plus, at home I miss out on the *musafaha*.

Tahajjud: Likewise, I've been quite lazy about praying in Dar al-Zahra, simply because we all do it at home. Only one of us, Eva, actually goes there every night. And again, the *'ajr* I would get if I go is a lot, so I'll try and go as often as I can.

But I am really happy that I am getting up every day for Tahajjud. They say that if you can do something for forty days or stop something for forty days, it becomes a habit or you get out of one. So insha'Allah not waking up is a habit I want to break and waking up is a habit I want to cultivate. They say the student of knowledge who doesn't wake up for Tahajjud is one you should "wash your hands of, for he is not a true student."

The Lives of Man: Really interesting. To think that our life here in this world is only one of five stages in our lives.

The Beginning of Guidance: An incredible class. We are studying all the sins the seven major body parts can do, and so far we've been studying the most dangerous one - the tongue.

Tawheed: The second most abstract class. It talks about the Oneness of Allah and His characteristics. Difficult, but you force yourself to concentrate more once you realise that the book we are studying was written for third graders (at the time the author, Habib Umar's father, was alive).

Hadith: We've probably all studied the Forty Hadith, but again I am getting so many insights from this class. Probably the class that feels most like a university class - we even have a syllabus!

Da'wah: Only had two classes so far; I'll elaborate more in a week, insha'Allah.

Seerah: I will never tire of hearing stories about the Prophet Muhammad ﷺ.

Thought: While praying Fajr today we heard an announcement of someone's death. That's how they do it here - the family uses the radio to announce who died, when they will be buried, and where the funeral will be. A good reminder that one day we will all die. The Prophet Muhammad ﷺ said that we should mention death every single day, ideally at least twenty times a day. There's a hadith quoted in *The Beginning of Guidance* that says:

"The Messenger of God said, 'Remember often the Ender of Pleasures.' He was also asked, 'Shall anyone be resurrected among the martyrs who is not one of them?' and he replied, 'Yes, those who remember death twenty times each day and night.'"

Today's Quote: "You take medicine that tastes horrible in order to get better and slave away at a job to get money. So why not endure difficulties to discipline your self?" (*Habib Umar*)

Day 17: Locked Out

We got locked out of the house today at noon, when the sun was at its peak.

Yesterday, we had an optional question and answer session with Shaykh Omar, our *fiqh* teacher. I was really thinking of skipping it, but eventually decided to go. I left early but ended up walking for half an hour in the heat from Dar al-Zahra to Habib Umar's house to the men's house (where the class was held) and back home before I realised the class was cancelled. Truly, I felt that that was a sign from Allah - kind of like: you were going to the class but weren't approaching it like a true student of knowledge should, so it got cancelled and you ended up walking in the heat.

Well, the session was rescheduled to today, and today I and three others decided to miss the class - the very first time I've skipped a class, even one of the optional ones other than the one about raising your children in the West. And the result? I ended up *boiling* outside the house.

Truly, it was a test in patience and 'holding our tongue' - what we've been studying in the *Beginning of Guidance* class for over a week - and I think all four of us failed miserably. I had asked my supervisor for the key before we made our way back home, and she had told me that there were two supervisors in the house. So I spent my time locked out complaining that she had told me there were people in there when there weren't. It was so hot my leather shoes were literally cooking my feet and none of us could even gather the energy to even *think* about walking back to Dar al-Zahra to find our supervisor and ask her for the key. We just kept ringing and ringing the bell, fanning each other with my pitiful mulan-style fan and complaining and complaining. The heat definitely brings out the worst in people.

Directly in our line of sight were men toiling in the earth, lifting heavy sacks and rocks and digging. And instead of looking at them and thinking how lucky we were to be currently sitting in the shade and soon to be sitting in an air-conditioned room, we just kept right on moaning.

↑ *Men working right outside the Dowra house*

Eventually, we remembered that instead of complaining, we should say alhamdulillah, and I remembered the story we were told just recently about the one-eyed man. So we said alhamdulillah, and I told them I hadn't done my *wird al-latif* today - since I was revising my Qur'an verses in the morning before class - so I got my MP3 out of my bag, pressed play, and literally all I heard was "Bism Allah al-Rahman al-Rahim" and the door opened.

A lesson well learnt!

Today's Quote: "It's ok to sometimes meander from the spiritual path. As long as you have a goal in mind, you can always get back to it, just like a car can get back on the road if it takes a right or left." (*Habib Umar*)

Day 18: Mirror

I got a text message from work today and it made me realise that I haven't had any 'contact' with the outside world in over two weeks. As a journalist, I read the newspapers every day, or at least skim the headlines and read any major stories. But I haven't done that in quite some time and I realise that I don't really care. Truly, here we are cut off from the 'outside world' - no phone calls, no internet and no newspapers. But I don't feel at all deprived, the world will still be the world when I get back home, and the news will still be the same. Paradoxically, things remain the same though the world itself may change drastically. On the other hand, I feel like the sun could rise and set for a hundred years and yet things will still be the same here in Tarim.

On a completely different note, we got two small mirrors in the house today. It's strange, but I don't use them at all. In the first couple of days when I got to Yemen, I thought I would go crazy without a mirror, asking to borrow one from anyone who had even a small compact one. So it's strange how quickly you get used to not checking yourself out in the mirror, and stranger still how quickly you get used to not worrying at all about what you're going to wear or what you look like.

My Qur'an teacher saw me yesterday and out of the blue asked me if I'd like to memorise *Surah Yaseen* instead. Initially I was like, "Phew, now I only need to learn one and a half pages a week instead of three," but then I thought that no, I'd decided to learn *Surat al-Kahf* so I was going to stick with that, even though it's a bigger challenge. I saw her again today and she told me that Habib Umar said that I should not memorise *Surat al-Kahf*, and instead memorise *Surah Yaseen*. So I'm guessing that's what I'm going to be doing now. But insha'Allah I'll get the reward of *Surat al-Kahf*, since that was my original intention.

Speaking of Habib Umar, we get so many dates from him in our morning class that each one of us can follow the *sunnah* (Prophet's ways and manners) and take seven, and still have enough left over. Again, the hospitality of the people here is overwhelming.

Day 19: Prophet Hud عليه السلام

Today we went to visit Prophet Hud ﷺ, known in the Old Testament as Eber, whose grave is an approximately ninety-minute drive from Tarim.

Before we went, we were told so many stories about him and about how it's a rite of passage for young boys to go on a trip there with a male relative when they're six or seven. In Sha'ban, the month before Ramadan, the entire city of Tarim makes a *ziyara* to his grave and spends up to a week there; the men go one week, the women another. And when the men come back, the women greet them dressed up, with *henna* decoration on their hands to celebrate their safe arrival. Basically, it's a big ritual to honour the Prophet Hud ﷺ. It's a trip that one prepares for and is not an easy one to make - there's even an intention specifically written in al-Habib Muhammad (Sa'ad) bin 'Alawi al-'Aidrus's *Book of Intentions* for those who want to visit the grave.

↓ *Crack in the mountain where it is said Prophet Hud ﷺ entered*

Prophet Hud's ﷺ grave is located up a mountain, since that is where he died. It's said that his *qawm* (people) were chasing him, and the mountain cracked open for him (you can actually see the crack). He entered the mountain and stayed there until he died.

It is also said that Prophet Hud ﷺ and his people were giants, and from how tall his body is, that definitely seems to be the case. Directly underneath the dome is where his head is located, and his body extends all the way out of the dome. It ends at the white stone. Subhan Allah.

↑ *Prophet Hud's ﷺ grave from the outside*

After we finished our *ziyara* we walked down the mountain to a shaded alcove and had our breakfast there. The view from there is stunning and it truly felt like a picnic.

→ *View from the alcove*

Next, we made our way over to the river which runs directly underneath the mountain - one of Prophet Hud's ﷺ miracles. The area was simply desert land and when his people asked him to give them proof that he was a prophet, the desert turned into a river. We're in summer now though, so the river was dried up for the most part. Unfortunately we were in a hurry so we didn't get to swim in the river as previous Dowra participants have been able to, but a lot of us dipped their feet in and squished their way back to the bus all muddy.

↑ *River at the bottom of Prophet Hud's ﷺ tomb*

I'm not feeling very articulate today - I fell down the stairs and I think I got a little too much sun - so forgive me for not being able to accurately portray the experience.

On our way back to Tarim we got to see children swimming in wells, palm trees as far as the eye could see, and camels chilling by the side of the road - one was crossing the road and the bus had to literally stop for him.

We also stopped at the grave of Shaykh Abu Bakr bin Salem on our way back, who was a great lover of Prophet Hud ﷺ. He even had a small room built next to the dome where he used to come to contemplate and reflect for up to three months at a time. We didn't get to go to his house though, so I was lucky to not only visit his grave a second time, but also his house.

Day 20: No Boys

It's the weekend again (where does the time go?!) and today we went back to the pool for another chill-out session.

This time, the men were also swimming in a pool within hearing distance (we could hear them all whooping and cheering) and I realised that I hadn't talked to 'boys' in almost three weeks. It's strange, but I don't really miss them. I mean, it's strange not interacting with men in the same sense that walking in the street and rarely seeing cars is - it's unusual but you get used to it. I thought it would be hard to see, live, and interact only with women, but it turns out I'm more adaptable than I thought.

Day 20 (Cont'd): Rain

It rained hardcore today around 'Asr time, just after I finished writing the previous entry.

Subhan Allah the weather changed in an instant. I was asleep the first time it rained while I was here, so I didn't know it could be like this. I've seen it rain buckets before in England, but this was a rain that rivalled even that rain, simply because of its rarity. It got gloomy, the temperature dropped, and the sky opened.

I went up to the roof and it was raining so much I could literally wring my *abaya* from how wet I got. I relished the rain and the big, fat, cold water droplets - how is it that an hour before it was so hot you could fry an egg on your face and then suddenly get so cold you're chilled? There was no lightning, but thunder rumbled over and over again, and somehow it seems so much more majestic when you're surrounded by mountains on all sides.

People all around us were up on their roofs - some turning their faces upwards towards the rain, others lifting their hands towards the sky and making *du'a* and others still being more practical and using the water to clean the roof. We, on the other hand, got a tambourine and starting singing *Tala'al badru 'alayna*.

→ *Children playing in puddles of rain and mud*

↑ Children playing in puddles of rain and mud

And then fifteen minutes later, it stopped as suddenly as it had begun, a wind began blowing, and the temperature climbed back up. I went outside and it smelled like rain and dust. All the sand had turned to mud, and children had all gathered to play in it.

A thought just occurred to me - it rained today on day 20, the day we crossed the half-way line. Half my time in this idyllic place is over. The moon today is also a full moon - when we came it was still a crescent, I remember looking at it when I was in Habib Umar's house in the mountains and thinking of how the month was still beginning. Time goes by, unlike what Madonna thinks, *so fast*.

Day 20 (Cont'd): Community Dinner

Today after the *mawlid* and 'Isha prayer, we were invited over to the home of one of the Western women who lives here for a community dinner.

Wallahi (I swear), we had so much fun. My expectations were two-fold: either no one would dress up or everybody would be incredibly dressed up like we do back home with women-only parties, but thank goodness it was somewhere in the middle. No one was dressed up, but for once, everyone was wearing colours, which was a wonderful thing to see after the black, black, black everywhere.

We were sitting on the roof, and the rain early this morning made the air incredibly fresh and fragrant to breathe. The full moon was beautiful.

A small group of women had been hired I guess to play the *duff* (a kind of drum/tambourine that some say is the only permissible instrument for Muslims to use) and sing *nasheeds*, and it really set the mood.

It was really inspiring to meet all the Western women who are living here. I notice that a lot of them have really young children - it'll be interesting to see how these first generation Tarimi Westerners turn out and what they'll do when they eventually go back to their countries.

So a great night overall - wonderful food, wonderful tea, wonderful hospitality, and a great end to our day off. A little girl gave us lessons in playing the *duff*; we sang *nasheeds* together, and we got an informal class in Tarimi dance.

Day 21: Lizard Adventure

You'd think mature, grown up, talented and worldly women would be quite capable of dealing with a tiny lizard, but no - our experience with the lizard was harrowing enough to deserve an entry all on its own.

So I go up to my room only to find four girls in it armed with brooms and mops eyeballing a tiny lizard perched on the ceiling, and glass all over my suitcase - they broke the fluorescent light fixture trying to guide the lizard to the open windows. Thing is, there are quite a lot of broken windows around the house, so it's not at all strange that something crawled its way in - probably because of the rain.

Eventually, more and more girls come to the room, drawn by the noise, and soon there are ten of us trying to direct the three that were brave enough to try and capture/kill the lizard.

The ceilings here are quite high - approximately four metres. So the girls ended up having to jump to try and push the lizard off the ceiling. Only it was so fast it kept scampering around the ceiling, which of course resulted in a corresponding scream and shuffle from the girls who then happen to be directly under the lizard.

Eventually, one brave soul managed to pin the lizard in place using the squeegee (the bathroom wiper kind of like what we use to clean windows), except she ended up only cutting off its tail (which fell on my suitcase!) and having the lizard twitch manically. *That* image has been seared in my brain.

So understandably, the lizard gets more agitated and scurries around the room like someone is chasing it (which, of course, someone is). One of my roommates decides that's it - she's moving out of the room and even shifts her mattress and bag out into the corridor.

But alhamdulillah, using the coordinated efforts of two girls, who manage to corner the lizard using a broom and a squeegee, the lizard is pushed down to a wall, and then a bucket was quickly put over it to stop it running away.

Then the search began for something to slide between the bucket and the wall so when the bucket was lifted the lizard wouldn't just jump straight out. My cornflakes box was deemed the most suitable, and in seconds it was torn apart and placed between the bucket and the wall.

Now we come to the most delicate part of the situation - tossing the lizard out of the window. But it seems the experience was too harrowing for the girls holding the bucket, who instead of just removing the makeshift cornflakes lid, decide to throw the entire bucket out of the window instead.

Mission accomplished. It only took twenty minutes, four girls, a can of insect spray, a chopped off tail, a broken light fixture, a torn up cornflakes box and a tossed bucket. Poor hapless lizard. Half an hour of fighting for its life, and it came out of it with no tail. But at least it lives another day. I just hope the goats don't eat it.

Day 21 (Cont'd): Tea Ritual

Today my family was invited for lunch at a Yemeni family's house in 'Inat. And not only did I get to enjoy another traditional Yemeni meal and visit Shaykh Abu Bakr bin Salem's grave for a *third* time (I also met a girl from Dar al-Zahra there, what are the chances?), but I also learnt a few more things about Tarim:

- I will never get used to going to the bathroom in a hole in the floor, the heat, the *niqab*, sitting on the floor, or wearing *hijab* twenty-four/seven like the women do here - even when they're sleeping!
- Little babies here are made to wear bracelets and anklets to "take away the eye" from them.
- For the heat, people have a stack of fans in their homes that resemble little straw flags on a stick.
- Yemeni people sit on the floor in the strangest way - their knees are contorted in a weird looking yoga pose. I guess it comes from sitting on the floor for so long.
- The electricity is cut off at least once a week here.
- People don't use soap here, instead they fill a little bowl with detergent and use that instead.
- Some of the old traditional houses have old doors that are still in use - and their lock and key is one of the strangest I've ever seen.
- Houses are very, very sparse, no matter what social class you come from. Here, houses are not supposed to be hotel-like, they're just places where you eat and sleep.
- Extended families can all live in one house and it seems pretty normal to them, even the fact that there are a minimum of a dozen children running around.
- Children here play with *sawareekh* just like Egypt - mini rockets that are like firecrackers but a bit more dangerous.

But the most interesting thing I got out of today was a lesson in the 'tea ritual' which is complicated enough to rival the Chinese one.

Tea here is not a Lipton tea bag, a spoon of sugar and some hot water that takes two minutes to make like it is back home - it's ceremonial and ritualistic and can take up to an hour to make.

↑ *Goats walking around Tarim*

→ *Equipment used to make Tarimi tea*

On the far left with the handle is the bucket of coal. Next to it is the water jug. Above it is the container where you pour any excess water. The bucket in the middle with the kettle on top is full of water and has holes at the top. What happens is that this bucket is plugged in to heat the water so it evaporates and the steam heats the kettle, which is full of tea and a bit of water. It takes approximately thirty minutes and is faster with the electronic 'bucket' - alternatively, you can heat the bucket with coal, which takes longer.

The four jars on the far right are full of three different types of tea – normal red tea, green tea, and a mixture of Nescafe and creamer – and sugar. In the centre is a bowl to put in all the little cups of tea and spoons and tiny trays after they are used - they are under the blue towel on the far right. In the centre at the front are lots of little jars of sugar to give out when you give out the tea, in case anyone wants more sugar.

So how it works is that the person in charge of this delicate process pours a little of the tea from the kettle into a cup followed by water from a tap in the bucket of hot water that's evaporating. She then puts sugar on each cup and it on a tray with little spoons, and then someone goes around with the tea cups and puts each one on an individual little tray. This process is then repeated at least a couple of times, since no one drinks just one cup of tea.

Unfortunately, the downside of my visit today is that I missed the *burda* recitation (Poem of the Mantle, an ode praising the Prophet) in Habib Umar's house, and something else which I still don't know what it was since I haven't gone back to the Dowra house yet. *Ma'lesh* (never mind), I guess it wasn't meant to be.

Today we also got to visit Dar al-Mustafa in the morning during Dhuhr time when the men were all out. And apart from being quite a bit bigger than Dar al-Zahra with not-as-good air conditioners (but then again it is twice the size with the same number of ACs), it was pretty much the same. I got to pray in the *mihrab* (prayer niche in the wall) where Habib Umar prays and gives his lectures.

↓ *Inside Dar al-Mustafa*

Today's Quote: "People give credit to those who only do what they have to. I've heard people say, 'Mash'Allah, this woman is so religious, she prays and she wears *hijab*!' or 'This man is a shaykh; he has a beard and he prays all his prayers in the mosque!'" (*Shaykh Imaad*)

Day 22: My Tongue

I just found out that all I missed yesterday was the *burda* reading and recitation of the *awrad* (litanies) in Habib Umar's house. I then realised something about myself.

In the last entry, I made it seem as though I didn't mind the fact that I'd missed out on something, and that I was ok with it. But because I thought I'd missed out on a trip to Seiyun - since that's where all the men went yesterday for a *mawlid* - I was actually cranky and irritated, and took it out of my family, who I was spending the night with. My mood only changed when I realised I didn't miss much.

Part of the trip here is learning to recognise your faults and beginning to change them. Well, today I realised that a big fault of mine is that I take out my frustration on those closest and dearest to me when I'm angry/sad/annoyed etc. even when it's not their fault. I complain, I frown, I moan, and basically, I am not a happy cookie.

I can have a really acid, acerbic tongue. As a teenager, I used to have a horrible temper; everything would push my buttons and I'd find myself lashing out at everyone, not even able to articulate the reason for my rage. My bad feelings would surge, swirling to the surface and I would find it near impossible to wade through them and pinpoint why exactly I was so mad.

It sounds really, really over the top when I read over what I just wrote, but truthfully that's how I was. Alhamdulillah I learned - just like the Beast did - that I 'MUST control my temper'. I mastered that aspect of myself, for the most part.

Now, I'm just sarcastic and mean and I can say biting hurtful things - even if they're truthful - that I later regret. I become severely critical and judgmental and pass on my observations in a scathing tone, literally flaying whoever happens to be in my path with my tongue.

A lot of my housemates were commenting on how so far, the Dowra seems to be focusing on two topics that come up in every single class in one way or another: intentions and the tongue. And subhan Allah, they are things I struggle very much with. Without correct intentions, your good actions are worthless, and as Prophet Muhammad ﷺ says, the tongue is the reason most people won't end up in paradise. (The full hadith, which ends with, "Is there anything which topples people on their faces into the Hellfire other than the jests of their tongues?" is number 29 in Imam Nawawi's Forty Hadith.)

So with regards to my tongue, I need to: find an outlet for my frustration; learn how not to take it out on innocent family members; and learn how to have *rida* (contentment), even if things don't turn out the way I want them to.

Prophet Muhammad ﷺ said:
"The most complete in faith are those best in character and kindest to their families." (*Al-Tirmidhi*)

Today's Quote: "If you want to know your station with Allah, look at His station with you." (*Habib Umar*)

Another Quote: "If someone gives you an expensive gift you thank them over and over again, but never thank God who's given you so much. God gives you so many blessings, we should thank Him. But we don't, and yet He gives us more. A mother gives up on her baby in an incubator after a while, God never gives up on us." (*Habib Umar*)

Day 23: Pizza Party

Today was an incredible day. Subhan Allah it wasn't at all planned but it turned out perfectly. I can't remember if I've ever mentioned this, but there is a group of around fifteen women from Belgium, Sweden and Denmark who are also here for the Dowra. They're staying in a separate house so we don't really have a lot of interaction with them, and some of them were only here for three weeks, which means that they're leaving tomorrow. So we decided to hold a pizza party for them. The programme was literally decided upon after Dhuhr, and mash'Allah the two who organised it did it perfectly. It ran as smoothly as if we'd been practicing for days. This was the programme:

> 9:30-9:35: Informal Welcome
>
> 9:35-9:40: *Nasheed: Tala'al badru 'alayna*
>
> 9:40-9:45: Recitation of Qur'anic verses and hadith (Arabic and English)
>
> 9:45-9:50: Cheerleader welcome!
>
> 9:50-9:55: Pep Talk
>
> 9:55-10: *Muslim Woman* [spoken word]
>
> 10-10:30: Dinner
>
> 10:30-10:35: Urdu *nasheed*
>
> 10:35-10:40: *I Love my Hijab* [spoken word]
>
> 10:45-10:50: *Nasheed: Ila Rasool Allah [All, except the Prophet of God]*
>
> 10:50-10:55: Closing speech by Ustadha Moneeba
>
> 11-11:15: Speeches by women leaving and *Hababas*

It's hard to explain why exactly this night was so special - it was just harmonious. It filled me with a sense of 'right-ness', like this was how entertainment was supposed to be. We were hospitable and smiling and more than that: genuine. We were genuinely happy to be hosting these women and entertaining them. Plus, it didn't feel like a waste of time - it felt like productive entertainment, if that makes sense.

The *duff* was beautiful, those who sang the *nasheeds* were beautiful, and so much effort went into the programme. Even the Urdu *nasheed* was translated into English and first read out to us. We were perfectly on time, which surprised me so much being that I'm used to running on AST (Arab Standard Time).

I still can't believe the cheer welcome, which was perfectly choreographed and just amazing (this is a what?! An 'E'. A what?! An 'E'. Oh! an 'E!' etc). Eight of my housemates basically spelled out 'Welcome' backwards.

One of my housemates who does counselling then gave us a short five minute talk on how Muslims in the 'West' think 'Eastern' Muslims are so backward when it isn't true.

I then performed *Muslim Woman*, which is a piece I'd performed a couple of months ago in a play held at my university. It's about a ticked-off woman mocking the stereotypes people have about Muslim Women. It was kind of nerve-wracking because it was a piece that was performed by four people so I had to quickly learn the lines of three others which I had only semi-learnt in rehearsals. My roommate Choclit (a convert who will soon celebrate her one-year anniversary of being a Muslim, so proud of her mash'Allah, she's an inspiration!) then performed this *incredible* piece she had written titled 'I Love my Hijab.' The daughter of one of the *hababas* who were invited then sang *Ila Rasool Allah* for us in a perfect nightingale voice.

Plus of course - we had pizza! I don't think that needs any elaboration. Suffice to say it was the home-cooked kind of pizza I usually don't go near at home but gobbled up immediately over here.

There are just no words to express the night. Truly fantastic. And after our guests went home we brought out the *duff* and sang the *Muhammadiya,* one of my favourite *nasheeds.* For some inexplicable reason, I'm walking on clouds tonight.

Today's Quote: "Saying 'I forgot my intention' is not an excuse for you. In fact, by saying it you're admitting that the world has overtaken you." (*Habib Umar*)

Day 24: Random Thoughts

- Today my roommate Lara and I performed our introductions. Basically, we have something in the house called 'the sisters' corner' and every day two buddies (we also have a buddy system - really not as corny as it sounds) get up and introduce themselves, what they do back home, why they came to Tarim etc. Only you don't introduce yourself - you introduce your buddy. So far it's been pretty interesting learning more about everyone else, especially since I wasn't in the Dowra house the first couple of days when everyone got to meet each other. Mash'Allah everyone is so accomplished.

  - Yesterday we got a new cook. Turns out he was supposed to be our original one and our food was supposed to be more diverse. So he's been trying to make it up to us with cornflakes, pasta, seasoned rice, and most memorably: beef teriyaki! I'm very happy with the new menu, but at the same time I'm very glad I had those weeks with more 'bland' food.

  - I also got to see the 'coffee' set yesterday, which looks very much like the tea set except this one had a pottery bowl over a bucket of coal. The coffee beans are first ground into fine powder and then passed around for everyone to smell and comment on before entering the next step of the process. It took forty minutes to make. Shame it tastes just like normal coffee.

  - Today we had a group of women come over to the Dowra house to teach us how to play the *duff.* I bought one, though it turns out I have no rhythm whatsoever.

- The rain a couple of days ago has driven a ton of insects into the house. Today we found a baby scorpion in Choclit's bag. And the wind has blown away our cardboard wall. (Explanation: the air conditioner is located where a door used to be; the door was removed and cardboard was put in its place. Still don't really understand why.) I sleep directly under the cardboard wall so I'm not exactly very happy.

Day 24 (Cont'd): Rawha Question

Today in *fiqh* class we finally finished the section pertaining to ablution and purification, which actually means we're on page 4 of the 33 page booklet. Subhan Allah, who would have thought we could spend so long just talking about ablution? Just goes to show how much we don't know.

Anyway, Shaykh Omar also gives an optional question and answer session once a week. The one question that resonated with everyone today was, "The *rawha* with Habib Umar is really deep. But how do we go about implementing Habib Umar's advice without getting overwhelmed by how horrible we are? (i.e. the deficiencies in our character)."

You could just see everyone nodding and smiling. Because it's so true. I come out of the *rawha* feeling like an insect and so despairing of ever fixing the faults of my character.

On the back cover of the book we are studying in the *rawha* are these verses of poetry by Imam al-Haddad that serve as a tiny fraction of what we try and remember every day - that all our desires and wants are focused on the wrong things. I've tried to translate them as best I can, but of course they sound totally different in Arabic. Forgive my poor translation skills:

Oh servant of the Body, how you strive to serve it,
Are you asking profit from what you can have only loss?
Advance towards the Self and complete its virtues,
For you are human [because of] the self and not the body.
Let your heart leave the world and its ornaments,
For when you sieve out [all the good in the world] you get only grief, and [when it's at your feet] it still leaves you.

Shaykh Omar's advice was:
1 Always renew your intentions;
2 Make sure to act upon the knowledge you receive;
3 Try and be completely content with what Allah has given you;
4 Keep listening to lectures like the *rawha* when you get back.

On a completely irrelevant note, I just discovered today that the men don't wash up or serve themselves in the male Dowra house. And they have curtains. No comment! (Not to mention the fact that their house is two minutes away from Dar al-Mustafa while ours is at least a five minute walk from Dar al-Zahra (though to be fair, we do have a microbus most of the time).

Today's Quote: "Just like you die if you stay three days without water, your heart will die if it stays three days without listening to anything that reminds you of Allah, whether it is Qur'an recitations or lectures. So what if you're not only not listening to things that remind you of Allah, but listening to things that make you forget Him?" (*Habib Umar*)

Another Quote: "Every time you sin layers are added to your heart, until eventually your feelings [towards Allah] are blocked. Every time you feed your body what it wants, it just wants more. And when you do that your soul is dying. If it could talk to you it would tell you to feed it; the food of souls is worship." (*Shaykh Imaad*)

Day 25: Death

Today we had an optional class about washing and burying the dead. It was for those who follow the Hanafi school of thought so I'll wait until they hold one for the Shafi'is, but in the meantime I read the short book they were studying: *What to do when a Muslim Dies.*

Truly the book, as short as it was, made me think. And particularly goosebump-inspiring for me was this:

"It is also recommended that those who are near the grave put three handfuls of dust on it, saying with the first: *'From it did We create you'*; with the second: *'To it shall We return you'*; and with the third: *'And from it shall We bring you forth another time.'*" (Surah Ta-Ha 20:55)

Strangely reminiscent of 'Ashes to ashes, dust to dust,' right?

A few entries ago, I remember I talked about how Prophet Muhammad ﷺ recommended that we mention death at least twenty times a day. In principle, it seems easy, but today when I remembered it just twice it was hard enough. The first time was in our *Lives of Man* class - today we finished the second stage of human life (this world), which ends with death. The second time was reading the book.

It seems morbid to tell yourself multiple times every day that one day you're going to be under the ground, all alone in the dark and being eaten by maggots, but in reality it's one of the best ways to force yourself into being 'good' and patient and content when you're not really feeling up to it. As Imam al-Ghazali advises: "Suppose that death is near and say to yourself, 'I shall endure the hardship today; perhaps I will die tonight,' and 'I shall be patient tonight; perhaps I shall die tomorrow.'"

Farshi al-turab (dust is my bed) is one of the best *nasheeds* I have ever listened to, speaking about death. Subhan Allah it really makes me ashamed of myself. If someone tells you that you have twenty-four hours to live, what would you do in those twenty-four hours? Chances are, not what you do every day. So technically, that's what you should do every day - live each day as if it was your last. And remember that:

"Wheresoever you may be, death will overtake you even if you are in fortresses built up strong and high." (Surat an-Nisa 4:78)

It's strange, but that verse just reminded me of a story I read when I was a little girl and for some reason I've never forgotten – *The Man who Wanted to Live Forever*. Basically, this is the story:

There was once a man who wanted to live forever. He asked the oldest man in his city how to do so and was advised to go to the Old Man of the Forest.

So he went to the Old Man of the Forest and asked him how long he would live for. The Old Man of the Forest said, "I will live until the last tree in this forest falls down." The man said that wasn't good enough for him so the Old Man of the Forest advised him to go to the Old Man of the Lake.

So the man went to the Old Man of the Lake and asked him how long he would live for. The Old Man of the Lake said, "I will live until this entire lake dries up." The man said that still wasn't good enough for him so the Old Man of the Lake advised him to go to the Old Man of the Mountain.

So the man went to the Old Man of the Mountain and asked him how long he would live for. The Old Man of the Mountain said, "I will live until this mountain falls down." The man said that was good enough for him and decided to live with the Old Man of the Mountain.

Hundreds of years went by, and eventually the man felt nostalgic and wanted to visit his home. The Old Man of the Mountain begged him not to go, telling him that everyone he loved had long died. The man insisted so the Old Man of the Mountain told him to go but to never get off his horse.

So the man went back, found out that everything has changed and eventually turned back to go home to the mountain. On his way, he comes across an old man sitting next to an overturned wagon of shoes. He stops to help him and the old man comes closer to him and puts his hand on his arm.

The man feels a shiver go down his spine and looks at the old man. "Who are you?" he asks. The old man replies, "I am death, and these are the shoes I have worn out running after you."

↓ *Shoe stand at Dar al-Mustafa*

It's strange that I've never forgotten that story. I even remember the last picture frame - the old man was dressed in a brown monk-like robe and his face was hidden like the Scream guy, with long wrinkled fingers.

So, on an even more cheerful note to end on, in *Lives of Man*, we are constantly reminded of the shortness of our lives, and even told that a poet once said:

"If a youth has nothing to boast of when he reaches twenty years, he'll never have anything to boast of."

Today's Quote: "There's no shame in taking from the world, only in making it an obstacle between you and God. Only take from the world what you need but don't love it. Just like you need to go to the bathroom but you don't love it." (*Habib Umar*)

Day 26: Time

Today is day 26, which means we only have exactly fourteen days left before we have to go back to our homes and lives.

Time flies. It really does. To be honest, I wasn't expecting that it would; I thought I was going to find the programme really difficult and start counting down the days somewhere in the middle. But alhamdulillah, the hardship has definitely not been as hard as I was expecting, which is a relief in some ways and a disappointment in others.

So since I was talking about a cheery subject yesterday, I may as well continue on with another cheery one: time.

I'm reading a book right now that belongs to our house supervisor titled *The Value of Time,* by Shaykh Abd al-Fattah Abu Ghuddah. It's basically a collection of very short stories (most just a couple of paragraphs long) about scholars of the past and how they valued their time. One, for example, would grind his bread into mush so it would be easier to swallow and he didn't waste time eating; another read continuously while he was walking; while yet another didn't attend the burial of his son so he wouldn't miss a class.

The book tells you that any time spent not seeking knowledge is wasted time. Not only do we waste time not seeking knowledge, but we waste it in ways that aren't even productive. So you could say I'm working to make a living for my family, and that would be a legitimate excuse for not seeking knowledge. But no, our excuses for not seeking knowledge aren't even justifiable. We sometimes even purposely look for ways to waste it! Ahmed Amin, an Egyptian author, once said:

"Time is life, and killing time is killing life."

How many of us have thought of that while we look for ways to 'kill time'? Even if we're not wasting time online, watching movies, listening to music etc., and instead working/studying etc (i.e. being 'productive'), how much of that effort is going to benefit us solely in this world and how much will also benefit us in the next?:

"If however you have uselessly neglected yourself as the animals do, not knowing what to do each hour, then most of your time will have elapsed fruitlessly and your life will have slipped from you [...] Do not be like the poor deluded fools who are delighted every day at the increase of their wealth and the decrease of their days. What good is there in increase of wealth while life is decreasing?" (*Imam al-Ghazali*)

A friend of my mother's calls this world *mobile haqeer* (a worthless mobile phone). The story behind it is that her son once told his father he wanted one of those fake mobile phones. His dad told him that he had a real mobile phone, why did he want a fake one, a *mobile haqeer*? The boy answered that he knew he had a real phone but that he still wanted that *mobile haqeer* - worthless in the grand scheme of things.

From then on, we've used *mobile haqeer* as a catchphrase for this *dunya* (world) - it's simply a *mobile haqeer*, and a poor substitute for the Hereafter, so why do we care so much about it? Of course, *mobile haqeer* is just a synonym for "gnat's wing" which is what the world is to Allah. In fact, it's worth less than a gnat's wing, and if it wasn't, as the hadith says, then Allah wouldn't have allowed the unworthy to even drink a cup of water from it:

"If this world were worth a gnat's wing before Allah, He would not give a disbeliever a drink of water." (*Al-Tirmidhi*)

Habib Umar illustrated this concept by saying:
"Imagine if you walked around with a fly and showed it to everyone telling them, 'I own a gnat's wing!' What will they think of you? And the whole world is worth even less than that."

I mentioned yesterday that in *The Lives of Man*, we are told that if you haven't accomplished anything by the age of twenty, you'll never accomplish much. Well, we're also told in the book that by the age of forty, you should seriously start contemplating your death and focusing only on Allah - because the age of forty is:
"... the pivot, the turning point, after which one's life in general works out the consequences of how one's soul was shaped during one's youth."

Oscar Wilde said that, "... by the age of forty, every man has the face that he deserves."

But then when I think of life today - how many forty-year-olds have accomplished all that they need to? It seems as though it is taking us longer and longer to 'grow up'.

Prophet Muhammad ﷺ said:
"The child is the master for seven years; and a slave for seven years and a vizier for seven years; so if he grows into a good character within twenty-one years, well and good; otherwise leave him alone because you have discharged your responsibility before Allah." *(al-Mukaram al-Akhlaq)*

It was explained by Imam Ja'far as-Sadiq as:
"Let your child play up to seven years; and keep him with you (for education and training) for another seven years; then if he succeeds (well and good); otherwise, there is no good in him."

One of the meanings I get from the hadith is that at the age of twenty-one, you're supposed to be fully mature and capable of living on your own and starting your own family. But today, we don't graduate from university until our early twenties, many don't think of marriage until their early thirties, and many at forty are still acting as though they were twenty.

Habib Umar, with all his vast knowledge and experience is only forty-three. Habib Ali is even younger - thirty-six. Yet they have accomplished so, so much. When I put it in that context, it seems so childish of me when I say, "I'm only twenty-one, I'm still young" as an excuse because twenty-one is old enough to have achieved so much more than I already have. It's just the time we live in that makes us spoiled and keeps us 'children' for a lot longer than we should.

Ahmed Shawqi, a famous Egyptian poet, once said:
"One's heartbeats say to him:
Life is but minutes and seconds.
Hence build for yourself a legacy after its death
For a man's legacy is his life."

It's strange that we always think that we have so much time left to grow up, mature, become religious. But our lifespans are tiny, compared to what they used to be. Prophet Nuh ﷺ - who lived at least one thousand years and fifteen hundred years by some accounts - said, when told that there would come a time when people would only live sixty years, that if he was them he would go and sit next to his grave.

And yet we still think that sixty years or so is an incredible amount of time. Even if you don't believe that people used to live for hundreds of years, just compare your lifespan to that of things on this earth - mountains and trees, for example, and you'll realise what a small lifespan it is. But because it's all we know, we think it's a lot. Someone once said that:

"The *adhan* is made in the baby's ear at birth, while the prayer is delayed until his death [Note: the funeral prayer has no *adhan*]. A sign that his life is short, just like the time between the *adhan* and the prayer."

There's this one episode of *Stargate* (yes, Stargate, I know) I saw when I was young and I have never forgotten. In it, the heroes visit a planet where someone messed up the inhabitants' genes so that they only lived for a hundred days. The heroes, of course, were aghast, indignant at how this person could have 'cheated' these people of their 'rightful' life spans. In the end, they fix the genes and go back happy.

But the interesting thing I found about the story is that the people on this planet weren't at all sad. They didn't think anything was strange about only living for one hundred days; in fact, they kept saying, "The creator has blessed us with a hundred days, for which we are grateful." To them, it seemed like such a long time, because that's all they knew. Even though to us it seems like such a limited amount of time, which if we knew we only had left we would definitely *carpe diem*, to them it was normal, and just the way things were. I wonder how we would live if someone told us we only had a hundred days left to live? I'm guessing like Prophet Nuh 🕊 thought about only living sixty years.

Today's Quote: "Whenever you start thinking that you have so much power and influence, think of this: The West, which seems so powerful, is actually in control of only half the land on this earth, which is only one-quarter of the entire earth - the rest is water. The earth is the third planet in a solar system, which is two million light years away from the nearest galaxy. One light year is 365 days x 24 hours x 60 minutes x 60 seconds x 300,000 km/s (speed of light). Think of two million light years. And then think that all these galaxies are only in the first sky. The seven skies are like a ring in the desert compared to the *kursi* (chair) of Allah, which, in turn, is like a ring in the desert compared to the *'arsh* (throne) of Allah." (*Shaykh Imaad*)

Another Quote: "When someone sick comes to you for advice, you don't tell him what medicine to take or perform surgery on him yourself, you give him the name of a good doctor. So why is it when someone comes to you for advice on a religious issue you immediately start giving your 'opinion'?" (*Shaykh Imaad*)

Day 26 (Cont'd): Library

Today we went to visit the library for Western children living in Tarim. Basically, it's just a small room with bookshelves split up into approximately a dozen categories. It's cute. There's a couple of books by Enid Blyton (and my favourite one of hers – *The Faraway Tree*), a couple by Roald Dahl, a couple by C.S. Lewis etc. Visiting the library and seeing how proud they were of the small collection of books made me realise how lucky I was. My library at home is at least twice the size of theirs, and I always complain about how I have no easy access to English books, since we don't have libraries in Cairo and there were no proper bookstores until a couple of years ago. So I would end up buying all my books from Amazon and alhamdulillah, I've built up quite a large collection which I never really appreciated until today.

I love books. Always have, always will. I've always thought it was a travesty that so few people really read any more. And I especially believe in the saying: "*Ummat iqra' la taqra*'": (The community of *Iqra'* [recite, the first word revealed in the Qur'an] does not read.)

I grew up on a steady diet of Sweet Valley Twins and Goosebumps books, and although now I don't think they're exactly the best things for young children to read, they turned me into a bookaholic who devoured books and read them from cover to cover. Now, I read at least a couple of books a week, anything I get my hands on - heavy socio-political texts, my little brothers' sci-fi books, newspapers, anything basically.

But since I've been here I haven't really read much. I finished reading all our assigned books the week I got them, and I've been filching books from my housemates but other than that I haven't really read anything. So when the librarian kindly allowed us to each borrow a book to read, I got really excited. I was really craving a book to read but at the same time I didn't want to waste my time here reading a children's fiction book or wading through a difficult adult biography of Malcolm X. In the end I decided on *Aesop's Fables*. I hadn't read them since I was in grade school and not only are they short and easy to read, but they're full of useful morals and lessons. And, as it says in the introduction:

"One might say that the fable created its own philosophy: the character of a being is its fate. [Aesop] realised long before Darwin that man is an animal and that his ideals, motivations, and rationalisations are nothing but a wolfish dialectic."

So in a curious way, it kind of meshes with what we're studying: changing your character and purifying your self.

Today's Quote: "People come to Tarim to escape from the pressures of their lives and to live an easier life in terms of spirituality. I don't want this for you. *La takoono farareen, koono qarareen.* [Do not be fleers, be those who come to prepare themselves to leave]." (*Habib Ali*)

Another Quote: "Most of us busy ourselves with *muhasaba* (critiquing) of other people who we will not be asked about in this life or the next - celebrities, football players and the like. These people do that and never *haseb* (critique) themselves once. This is the fool. He has files open for people and not one for himself. He should close those files and open one for himself, because if the entire world sins then it's not a problem for you, but one sin that you commit is a problem for you." (*Habib Umar*)

Day 27: Imam al-Haddad's Mosque

Today we went to visit the mosque and house of Imam Abd-Allah ibn 'Alawi al-Haddad. Just the thought that we were in the house of the Sufi Sage of Arabia, the man who wrote some of my favourite books, was awe-inspiring.

↑ *Outside of Imam al-Haddad's mosque*

↓ *Minaret at the mosque of Imam al-Haddad*

↑ *Inside Imam al-Haddad's mosque*

The mosque is pretty. Although it's very modern and recently rebuilt, it's still pretty. But more interesting was the *khalwa* (seclusion/worship area) at the back of the mosque, which is where the Imam used to sit and contemplate. Back there is also his rosary - which has a thousand huge beads.

← *The case where Imam al-Haddad's rosary is kept*

→ *View into one of Imam al-Haddad's tiny bedrooms*

But *most* interesting was his house. Truly, it was humbling to visit. It's tiny, even smaller than Shaykh Abu Bakr bin Salem's. It's literally minuscule and claustrophobic - the ceiling is extremely low and I banged my head into it twice going up (and down) the stairs. On the first floor are two tiny rooms, and I will never forget the size of his bedroom - it was literally the size of a single mattress. Each room is no bigger than three steps in any direction. On the second floor was the biggest room, which took up almost the entire floor: his lecture room for his students, which can't fit more than thirty.

→ *Imam al-Hadadd's lecture area*

For some reason, the second floor also contains a hook hanging from the ceiling, which we were told is where animals were slaughtered and hanged. I find that very disturbing for some reason - slaughtering animals inside a house?

Like I've said more than once, houses in Yemen are very, very basic, and that's because they're not supposed to be a 'haven', they're supposed to make you remember that life is fleeting and they're supposed to support an ascetic lifestyle, which means you're not supposed to be very comfortable in them. A far cry from our spacious homes. I have yet to visit a house here that has 'real' furniture in it - at most there is moquette fabric for the floor. If you peel it, you will literally see concrete underneath.

Another reason for the fact that there is no furniture is that everyone sits on the floor. And they sit on the floor because of the hadith that says:

"One who humbles himself for the sake of God, God will exalt him [in rank]." (*Imam Muslim*)

Prophet Muhammad ﷺ used to sit and eat on the floor. Once, a woman saw him eating on the floor and said, "He is eating as if he were a slave." The Prophet responded:

"Could there be a better slave than me? I am a slave of God." (*Haythami, Majma', 9.21*)

And so, the people of Tarim, even the shaykhs in our classes, sit on the floor.

But I digress. We sat in Imam al-Haddad's lecture room and recited his *wird*. I learnt what the word *wird* means today (it's weird that I never thought about that) - it means the well which waters the earth. So the *wird* waters your heart. And as Shaykh Imaad told us in a class, it doesn't happen automatically, you need to do it for a long time before you begin to taste it (*zawq*).

We then opened one of Imam al-Haddad's books and read the page it opened on. Subhan Allah it was so appropriate:
"*Iman* is like a tree. Faith is the roots and good character and deeds are the branches. Tribulations are like a flood or wind that hit the tree. If the roots aren't strong enough the tree might be uprooted." (*Imam al-Haddad*)

Then we opened his *qaseedas* and read the one the book fell open to, which he had written after he came back from Hajj, pilgrimage. Doing so is called *mashad*, witnessing – it's said that what the book falls open to describes your state.

All in all, our *ziyara* took two hours. Imagine meeting one of your favourite authors, and imagine being invited to their house. So I'm honoured to not only have been in Imam al-Haddad's house, but also to have visited his mosque *and* his grave (in Zambal).

Today's Quote: "Who doesn't have a *wird* is a *qird* (monkey)." (*Ustadha Moneeba, quoting a scholar*)

Day 27 (Cont'd): Goats

I saw a herd of goats and sheep cross the street right in front of me today, and I don't think I've ever seen so many of them in my life. Only this time they actually had someone leading them. For real, these goats just cruise and chill around Tarim, and you can just feel them thinking, "We own this city!"

↑ ↗ Goats in Tarim

Day 28: Women Scholars

In the beginning of the Dowra, I remember I said that I was really disappointed we couldn't talk or really 'see' the shaykhs, but today, I've re-thought that statement.

After a class with Habib Umar's wife yesterday, something hit me. Throughout the weeks we've been here, we have been able to meet all the *hababas*, something none of the men will ever get a chance to do.

Even though the men get to meet the shaykhs, realistically how often do they get a chance to sit with them, talk to them, and ask them questions? Probably not that often. They say that behind every great man is a great woman, and for Habib Umar, for example, we got to meet that woman (his mother), in addition to his wife, his daughters, and even his grandchildren. What's more, we get to sit with them, talk to them and interact with them - women scholars are generally more accessible and approachable than men, plus the amount of female students is smaller than the number of male students.

Habib Umar's wife - and I'm calling her 'his wife' and not by her name out of respect for the culture here which doesn't think it's proper to call women by their names but as 'the wife/daughter/ mother of' - is an incredible scholar with a lineage to rival any well-known male scholar. Her class was one of the most interesting ones I have listened to in this entire Dowra, and only women can take advantage of her knowledge. So we get the best of both worlds - listening to male scholars *and* listening *and* interacting with women scholars. Men, on the other hand, will probably only get to listen to male scholars.

And there *are* women scholars, unlike the misconception that they don't exist. And the best translator I've heard so far, out of all the ones we've listened to, was the female translator who translated for the female scholar we met in the very beginning of the Dowra (in the Western sisters' welcome) and yesterday for Habib Umar's wife.

As women, we get to meet women *walis* and have them make *du'a* for us. Today we visited two of them in their homes (they're alive), one of them the sister of a great shaykh, Abd-Allah al-Shattery, who had thirteen thousand students and never wrote books because he said he was busy preparing 'great men'.

And on that note, I wanted to explain a little bit why we visit these *awliya'*. The simplest explanation I can give is this: imagine if you were given the opportunity to meet someone who could possibly help you a lot in one aspect of your life, such as work. Basically - networking and having contacts. Well, *awliya'* are our networking and contacts, but not for this world. Prophet Muhammad ﷺ is said to have said that visiting them, even for the time it takes to cook an egg, is a great deed. So we visit.

Today's Quote: (After the electricity went out in yesterday's class): "The student who sweats in *majlis 'ilm* (knowledge gathering) will insha'Allah not sweat on the Day of Judgement [when some will be swimming in their sweat]." (*Habib Umar's wife, quoting a scholar*)

So I guess my decision to go to the *rawha* in Dar al-Zahra rather than sitting comfortably at home was a good one! And on that note, Shaykh Abd-Allah al-Shattery said that a *majlis 'ilm* was better than, "A thousand visits to sick people and attending ten thousand funeral processions."

Day 29: Dream

I woke up in the middle of the night today and couldn't sleep so I decided to go to the roof and sit in silence for a while.

I will miss this silence. Cairo, like a New York Times article says, is a city where you literally "can't hear yourself scream." The average noise in Cairo from 7am to 10pm is 85 decibels, a "bit louder than a freight train only fifteen feet away." In some ways, it's nice to live in anonymity in a big cosmopolitan city where you can get lost, but at the same time it must be nice to live in a place where you can tell the microbus driver (no cabs here) take me to so–and–so's house, and he knows automatically where it is. That's how small Tarim is. Sometimes, you just need silence to think. And what I thought about tonight is what I want to take back with me from Tarim.

My mother had a dream about me and had it interpreted by their neighbour (the elderly *habib*). She dreamt I was pregnant. In Arabic, the word pregnant, *hamel*, literally means 'the carrier', i.e. you are carrying a baby. Well, the interpretation she got is that the pregnancy symbolises the knowledge I have gained from this Dowra - which I will go back 'carrying'.

I'm still kind of sketchy about dreams - any dream you have you could say was a 'vision', how could you distinguish either or? Plus you can get a dozen different interpretations for the same dream. Either way, it's a beautiful interpretation, and I wish it was true. That I truly come back from this Dowra with knowledge that I carry and then pass on, but I'm not presumptuous or arrogant enough to think that. So for me at least, the dream was just a manifestation of my Arab mother's subconscious desire for me to get married and have children!

But it definitely is time to start thinking about going 'back': tomorrow (or today, as it may be) is day 30, which means three-quarters of my time here is up. We leave on Monday morning for Makalla/Al-Rayaan on a four day trip which I'm really excited about but sad at the same time because it means we'll only have six days left in Tarim when we come back.

I feel like I've taken root here. It's only been a month and yet the day now feels as natural to me as any jam-packed day I had back home. I've realised a lot about myself, good and bad, but I'm still not clear about what exactly my resolutions are for when I go back home, and what, if anything, I'm going to change about my life.

Ustadha Moneeba told us once that Tarim is like a well, and so we must take as much water from it as we can. So I'm taking in the water, but I'm not exactly sure if my container is good enough not to let the water drip out or evaporate. And even if it is, what am I going to do with the water?

Day 30: Choclit

I want to dedicate today's entry to my roommate, Choclit Angel, who's a twenty-three-year-old African-American who lives in Seattle and is studying journalism at the University of Washington (and yes, that is her real name).

Today, Choclit is celebrating her first anniversary of the day she became a Muslim. We're telling her happy birthday because it's almost as if she was reborn on this day. Just like we did with the Swedish sisters, we had a little pizza party for her, complete with the cheer welcome, just because mash'Allah this woman is incredible. We (actually it was just Sarah) also put together a slideshow of pictures of her and videos of all of us saying *mabrouk*, congratulations.

Choclit's awe-inspiring story, when she told it to me, just blew me away. It left me gob-smacked, impressed, and more than a little ashamed of myself. Choclit was the most popular girl in school, with the weave and the make-up and the big earrings etc. She was a cheerleader, a model, an actress, a pageant girl, a belly-dancer, and a Hooters girl, among other things (including being a Bible Studies leader). When you hear about how she *literally* gave up her life to become Muslim, it brings into sharp relief all the things we find so difficult to do and yet aren't a tenth as hard for us as they are for her.

A lot of what she told me I'm sure she doesn't want made public knowledge, but suffice to say she wasn't raised in the most fortunate of circumstances. When she became a Muslim, her parents and siblings didn't take her conversion to heart, and made life as miserable as they could for her.

She's only been Muslim for a year but subhan Allah she has been gifted with two incredible gifts - knowledge and incredible humility. She learnt more about Islam in a year than many of us learn in a lifetime. From knowing that the person who doesn't wake up for Fajr has the *noor* (light) removed from their faces, to the fact that a shooting star means a *shaytan* (devil) has just died, she knows a lot, mash'Allah.

She wore *hijab* the weekend she became a Muslim when a week earlier she was on stage dancing in a skimpy outfit. She's repeating some of her prayers because she says she was mixing up between Islamic schools of thought; something that definitely doesn't require you to repeat your prayers. She became the Public Relations Officer for MSA (Muslim Student Association) and wants to move to Berkeley to study Islam in the Zaytuna Institute.

She's a spoken word artist and managed to turn that around into a way to defend Islam. She performed this incredible piece in last week's pizza party titled, 'I Love my Hijab', which she wrote herself. It's heart-warming, inspiring, and makes you feel insect-like if she, a 'brand-new' Muslim, can be brave enough to defend Islam in an audience which isn't exactly forthcoming, what's our excuse?

And mash'Allah she doesn't think that any of this is amazing. When you ask her to share her story she just shrugs and says, "I was lost, and then I was found." She's incredibly brave and especially eloquent, and puts to words what so many of us may be too afraid to voice out. I quoted her earlier on as saying:

"The experience here makes me feel like the seven dwarves rolled into one. The heat makes me like grumpy and sleepy especially. I feel that you got stuck with me here, and that you're all so much better than I am. I'm scared to go back home and not have this aura of spirituality that everyone who comes here has when they go back to their homes, and to have people ask, 'Wait, wasn't she in Tarim?'"

You know what Lucas in *One Tree Hill* (yes, I know) said about Peyton in his book? It went something like this, "Peyton has the potential for greatness and she doesn't even know it." Substitute Choclit for Peyton and there you have it. I truly believe this woman is going to do great things, even if she herself doesn't believe that yet.

And although she can be grumpy and sleepy sometimes, as well as a scary antisocial 5'9 giantess (!), I love her for the sake of Allah. And though I may never see her again in this life, I hope to meet her under the shade of Allah on the Day of Judgement as two sisters who "loved each other for [Allah's] sake."

Happy Birthday Choclit, may it be the first of many.

Today's Quote: "If you have *zuhd* (renunciation of the world) you won't care about what people have, and will be able to look at what you have that others don't have, rather than look at what you don't have and someone else has." (*Shaykh Imaad*)

Day 30 (Cont'd): Bay'a

Something else happened today which I've been debating writing about because of the controversy surrounding it. But it's part of my experience here, and an important one, so I've decided to share it.

So I come back from Tahajjud and Fajr prayer at Dar al-Zahra only to be told that Habib Umar is going to give *bay'a* (covenant) to those of us who want to in half an hour.

It threw me for a loop, it really did. In its simplest terms, *bay'a* means you have chosen a shaykh and have "handed him your reins" to guide you on the spiritual path. You then become a *murid* (one who desires) who trusts his shaykh completely, follows his commands, recites the *awrad* you are given and from then on are 'connected' to this shaykh and his chain of teachers spiritually.

The concept is firmly rooted in Sufism. Personally, I love Sufis and I think they embody so many aspects of our religion that we can't even identity, let alone experience or understand. But like I said, I still don't know exactly where I stand on visions/dreams, which are supposedly a big part of how you connect with your shaykh.

Plus, choosing your shaykh is a big decision, and even though Habib Umar is an incredible shaykh, and I would be honoured to have him be my shaykh, am I sure that I'm even ready for one? And it's not like I can change my mind about it. A lot of people tell you that if you're not exactly clear about what a *bay'a* is or what it entails, you should choose the shaykh you feel the most connection too. And honestly, I have felt more connection with other shaykhs. So as bad as this sounds, I was kind of glad when the *bay'a* was postponed. Now I have time to do *istikhara*, a prayer where you ask Allah for guidance, and think.

Day 31: Hotel

We're in a hotel. The Hadhramaut Hotel. I feel as excited as a little child on Eid day.

The day started out with us leaving Tarim an hour later than planned, squished together like sardines in a crowded bus. As usual, we failed the test in patience, complaining about how the men's bus was so much emptier, and about how women always get the short end of the stick. So after a bit more moaning about the heat, the drive, the crowded bus, the *niqab* etc., we settled in for a couple of hours of sleep.

The further away we got from Tarim, the stranger the landscape became. I'd become so used to seeing humungous mountains and palm tree-covered valleys that the bare, flat, rocky landscape was somewhat strange and felt too exposed.

→ Flat, rocky landscape
on the way to Makalla

We made a pit stop to have breakfast (eggs that were somewhere between scrambled and omelette-y and tea with milk) and use the bathroom. (I have literally been scarred with my experience with the hole in the floor, I think I'm going to have nightmares about it from now on, no joke.)

We then continued on our journey, passing time (not killing it!) by playing 20Q and this strange game called Picnic which I still don't really understand. We then went back up the two lane road built into the humungous mountain I talked about in the very beginning of this book. Only this time I was fully awake and in more awe of creation than ever before.

Right before I came on the Dowra I had just come back from a conference in Norway, where every single mountain and fjord was literally covered with trees, to an inch. So to see that and then these majestic rocky mountains just fills you with wonder.

At the bottom of the mountain is a small valley filled with houses. It must be incredible to wake up every day and see mountains in every direction you look and palm tree-filled valleys on either side - definitely a big difference from waking up and seeing high rise buildings and paved streets, as far away from nature as we could possibly be.

→ *Going down the huge
mountain on the way to Makalla*

Eventually, after a seven hour trip on the bus with aeroplane economy size seats (and I thought six in a car was hard), we reached Makalla/Al-Rayaan. The sight of the coast on the horizon rejuvenated us all (and let me tell you, wild goats cruising on the beach look so out of place!), as did the beautiful weather, which was enough to revive anyone's spirits.

An hour later, we checked in.

Subhan Allah, the (mostly) ascetic lifestyle we've been living in for the past month made us appreciate all the little things we take for granted and that I know we'll go back to taking for granted once we go back home (I know I've said that more than once, but it's true).

I've stayed at Burj al-Arab in Dubai and yet I think I was happier entering this hotel room than I was entering that seven-star hotel. And do you know why?

- It has real, live beds! (said to the tone of "a real, live boy!" Pinocchio-style) with bouncy mattresses and not the hard-as-a-rock ones we've been sleeping on. With comforters!
- It has a real, live air conditioner! I don't think I've mentioned this before, but the air conditioners in Tarim are 'desert' ones that work with water and need a window or door open. I don't really understand the mechanics but they're really loud and although the air that's emitted is cool, it's just not the same as a 'real' AC. (Kind of like the difference between a bottle of water from a cool room versus a bottle of water from the fridge.)
- We have a shower! Where we can control the temperature and don't need to hold up the shower head because there's a place to hang it on!
- No hole in the wall! Which means no insects!

And so on and so forth. All the things you expect to find in a hotel room: soap, shampoo, a private fridge, a mirror hanging in the bathroom and a full length one in the bedroom, a wardrobe, chairs, curtains, little lava-lamp-looking lamps and a TV all filled us with glee because apart from the soap and shampoo, we'd been living without them for a month. And because it was so unexpected (last year all the Dowra sisters slept in one big room in a house so I was honestly picturing us in shacks on the beach), it makes it all the better. I feel like I'm on holiday!

And because we're coming here from a much less comfortable life, to us this is heaven. I was just thinking that if I'd come here straight from the airport, I wouldn't have thought that this two star hotel (ok, three star at best) was anything special, and in fact I would have probably only noticed the things it lacked. But now, you can tell that the hotel made us all as happy as little children. What makes me happiest is that the hotel is literally 'on' the seafront. Although the sea smells a bit like the kitchen of a seafood restaurant, the view outside the window is of the sea, and you can hear the waves crashing outside, which more than makes up for the smell.

Ever since I was a child, the summer holidays for me equals beach. As soon as school was out, my entire family piled into a car and headed out for the North Coast for at least a month, waking up just before 'Asr and going to sleep after Fajr, eating mangoes and spending all day in the sea.

But last year was my first year working and I spent my entire vacation time in the Rihla. This year, I took a leave of absence to attend the Dowra and I have to go right back to work the second I land back in Egypt. Which means I haven't *sayeft* (literally 'summered') in two years. So the sound of the waves crashing onto the big black rocks soothes me a whole lot.

↓ *Waves crashing on to the black rocks*

But I do envy the men, because of course as women we can't go swimming in the pool, scuba diving or swimming in the sea. A

lot of the men (from the Dowra) just jumped straight into the pool when they arrived - one of them was even wearing his trunks under his *jalabiya*!

But right now I am more than content to sit and watch the waves crashing on the shore and the sporadic lightning strikes.

Day 31 (Cont'd): Beach

We just came back from the beach.

I want to pause a bit and just look at that sentence. It sends a thrill of happiness throughout my body every time I read it.

Ok, so we didn't swim.

Ok, we went at night.

Ok, there wasn't any beach 'experience' (i.e. umbrellas, cocktail fruity drinks, music playing etc.)

But I had so, so, so much fun.

We weren't even told where we were going, just that we were going for a *jawla* (stroll). We thought that meant just driving around the city in a bus, and enjoyed it thoroughly for the first ten minutes, taking picture of the huge crowds of guys just chilling in the streets (truly, I don't think I've ever seen such a huge number of people with such a miniscule number of women). We also saw the river-looking-like sea. Basically they've somehow forced the sea into a channel so it looks like the Nile, kind of, but is really the sea. There was a silly moment when we thought we were going to this big market/tiny amusement park, but the real surprise was so much better.

The bus parked on the road, which had dozens and dozens of groups of men/families sitting outside their parked cars chilling in the breeze, eating/chewing *Qat*/listening to music. I even saw one guy sitting in front of a bonfire.

We then made our way to the beach and waded out into the sea. The feeling of the cool, squishy sand (a lot firmer than the beaches back home, though) was heaven, as were the waves crashing into us - the waves here aren't like the ones back home, which come one at a time, they crash four or five at a time. I'm glad we went at night - in the morning we probably wouldn't have been as free to go in as deep (knee height at least) and the sun would have been really intense.

We ran on the beach (the guys played football), wrote on the sand and took lots of pictures. But perhaps best of all, we saved a life.

So it was the life of a fish that lies on the bottom of the sea and that kept blinking at us, but still. It had been pushed to the shore by the waves and drying out. So like the Chinese fable of the whale, we began pouring water over it to keep it from drying out. It took the combined efforts of eight girls, the front and back covers of my notebook to slide under it to carry it (somehow, it's always my stuff that needs to be sacrificed), two electric shocks, and flipping the fish on its back a couple of times, but eventually we returned it to the sea to the sound of cheers and whoops from all of us. Mission accomplished.

On our way back, we stopped at a supermarket. And although it took us an hour because only two of us were allowed in (so those two had to make a huge list with what all twenty-five of us wanted, take our money, go and buy the stuff and separate each person's list and money) it was worth it. I am now the proud

↓ *Kiosk in Makalla's city centre*

owner of a Cadbury chocolate bar which I have been craving more than Charlie wanted that Willy Wonka bar, and half a dozen mangoes which I will savour.

Our room is all sandy now and I don't care. And even if I did, housekeeping will take care of it. And now to my fluffy, real live bed!

Day 31 (Cont'd): Burger

I just had a burger. With ketchup. And mayonnaise. And lettuce. And tomatoes. And French fries. And 7Up. And it got delivered like normal room service.

A real, live burger.

Day 32: Mango

Woke up today at 9am feeling like the laziest, most indulgent person in the world. Waking up when my body wanted to wake up is a luxury I haven't had for a while, since because of Tahajjud and the 5am class we don't have more than three uninterrupted hours of sleep at a time. But more than that, no one woke me up to tell me breakfast was ready, or the bus was waiting, or that I'd be late for class etc. And I didn't feel like the biggest sloth for sleeping as I usually do when someone passes by our room and looks in at us sleeping while they're up and about.

And now I just had a mango -"a real, live mango!" - eaten 'messy' style i.e. peeling the skin with your teeth in thin strips and only taking a humungous bite once you've peeled it completely.

I am so happy right now, hippy hoppy happy. And now it's time to get dressed and go to Shihr, where we're spending the day today and attending the big *mawlid* there for the *isra'* and *mi'raj* (the ascension of Prophet Muhammad ﷺ to the heavens), which is tonight.

Day 32 (Cont'd): Shihr

Bism Allah.

We set off for Shihr around noon and I decided to go with my family in their car so we could stop on the way and visit some more *walis* - Ibn Ismail and Ahmed ibn Mohammad al-Haddar. (The driver also had one of those weird fur things on his chair just like the driver who drove us to Tarim so I realised it must be a cultural thing.)

↓ *Mausoleum of Ahmed al-Haddar*

We drove through the *souq* (market) of Makalla, and it looked like a wannabe Khan el-Khalili/Souq el-Gomaa (the Egyptian equivalents of Portobello market), albeit with men playing cards rather than smoking *shishas* and playing backgammon.

← *Streets of Makalla*

↓ *Men selling fruit in the streets of Makalla*

↑ *Outdoor vendors in Makalla showcasing their wares*

→ *Man selling dates at the side of the street*

→ *Artifical river that runs through Makalla*

↑ *Fruit seller in Makalla*

→ *Kiosk selling random hygiene products and household equipment*

↓ *Headless palm trees on the way to Shihr*

The further away we got from Makalla, the more I realised how cosmopolitan it was (by Yemeni standards) - no mud houses in Makalla, and the *niqab* rule isn't as rigid (we rebelled a little bit yesterday and opened the door to the room service guy without it). After passing by a group of scary looking headless palm trees and a lot more beach-looking sand we made it into Shihr.

Shihr is a lot like Tarim, and in fact they call it the sister of Tarim (which is called the daughter of Madinah), as well as the city of *so'd* (happiness). Same mud houses and same stark environment, but minus the blistering heat and plus cute looking flowery curtains that look strangely out of place on the windows. It was actually unexpectedly windy there, and nice cool wind, not the hairdryer type wind we get in Tarim.

← *Houses in Shihr*

↓ *Setting up for a wedding in the streets of Shihr*

↑ *An all-male café in Makalla*

→ *Man selling siwaks at the side of the road*

Our first stop of the day was at the school of Khadija al-Kubra, named after Prophet Muhammad's ﷺ first wife. A teacher introduced the school to us: it was set up eight years ago, and the two hundred students are taught in six subjects. In those eight years, fifty students have learnt the entire Qur'an by heart, mash'Allah. The school was built to "revive hearts with the light of Islam," since after the British were expelled the country was under communist rule for a quarter of a century, which led to a deterioration in the understanding of Islam.

The teacher who explained this to us had beautiful Arabic skills. I know that's not linguistically correct to say, but it's the word that fits. Truly, Arabic is a beautiful, eloquent, expressive language. Compared to it, English is so restrictive and crude.

We were late so all the students had gone home, but we were greeted so, so enthusiastically by the teachers, who sang us up the stairs. I don't know if it's in the air or maybe because they've had so much practice, but almost all the women here have beautiful voices.

Subhan Allah they had prepared a whole programme for us and gave us VIP treatment. They welcomed us and performed a short piece for us in English (which I'm sure took them ages to prepare), sang us *nasheeds*, gave us dates that melted in our mouths and Tang-tasting juice, and fed us a feast of chicken and rice. They also gave each of us a green silk sash they had personally made, embroidered with yellow and with the *shahada* written in calligraphy on it. And on each one they had pinned a little piece of paper they'd laminated with ribbons hanging off it. The piece of paper said that this was a present from the school.

Again, as I've said so many times, I can't get over the kindness of people here; you will never feel like a stranger in this country, where people greet you like long-lost relatives.

We then made our way back to the bus and passed by a stage being set up for a wedding. This big group of women passed by us, and although they were all wearing *niqab*, you could see their made-up eyes with blue eyeshadow and dresses peeking out from under their *abayas*!

We then made our way to a huge courtyard, where Habib Umar was supposed to give us a lecture. We entered and (as bad as this sounds), my heart jumped - the sight of hundreds of women dressed from head to toe in black (with *niqab*) turning to see us enter was just scary. At the same time, it looked almost like something you'd see in a National Geographic picture.

As to why at least half the women were wearing *niqab* in a women only setting - it turns out in Shihr unmarried women don't show their faces to married women. And for some reason most of the women with uncovered faces had bright lipstick on.

But if everyone staring at us wasn't uncomfortable enough, Habib Umar's lecture was cancelled, and the women decided that some of us telling our 'stories' would be a good way to pass the time. Eva, bless her, was brave enough to get up, only she was too overcome to talk much. And mash'Allah some of the women started crying because she was crying, without even knowing her story or what she's gone through, calling her a *miskeena* (pour soul).

It's scary how hard and dead our hearts have become. It takes a lot to make me cry, and even then I wouldn't cry in public. I can't imagine my heart being so sympathetic and so unselfish that the pain of someone else could be reflected in me like a mirror.

After Eva finished, Ustadha Moneeba motioned to Choclit to come up, only she was too shy to go. So she motioned to me, and Choclit and I kind of encouraged each other to get up. Choclit told her story and I translated. And truly, speaking to those women was scarier than giving the graduation speech in my commencement ceremony to a couple of thousand people. Scarier than speaking in front of Habib Ali and Dr. Ramadan al-Bouti in the *Litaarafuu* conference in Abu Dhabi following the Danish cartoon crisis. It was scarier because it was a huge responsibility to try and faithfully convey to those women Choclit's story and her bravery in a way that would reach their hearts.

After that, we made our way over to the central mosque, where the *mawlid* was going to be held after Maghrib. I needed to renew my *wudu'* (ablution) and there was nowhere for women to do so in the mosque so one of the women took me to the nearest house and we knocked on their door. I'm trying to imagine someone knocking on my door and telling me they need the bathroom and what my reaction would be. Somehow, I don't think it would be "come right on in".

The *mawlid* began with a number of men giving short five minute lectures about the *isra'* and *mi'raj*. I was feeling kind of tired and was thinking of dozing for a bit when two of my housemates came to me and asked me if I would mind translating for them. I said ok, and I am *so* glad I did, because (and I say this because I know myself), if I'd let myself doze I probably would have missed half the lectures.

But because I was translating, I had to concentrate 150%. One, because the Arabic they were speaking was classical Arabic, and two, because the Yemeni accent is hard to understand. But even though it turns out there was a real translator who would have explained things to them so much better than I did, alhamdulillah, I think I did ok, and now I realise how difficult simultaneous translation is. And who would have thought that I could possibly translate one of Habib Umar's lectures (which was incredible by the way), which I could barely understand a month ago?

Unfortunately we had to miss out on the actual *nasheeds*, since they aren't going to start until after Fajr. We prayed 'Isha behind Habib Umar for the first time, and the girls then made their way back to Khadija al-Kubra (the school) to have a light supper, while I made my way back with my family so we could stop and get pizzas for everyone from Pizza Hut, the one and only fast food restaurant in the city! On our way back we passed over the bridge that overlooks the canal filled with sea water, and there was a concert with hundreds of men gathered - I'm guessing it was a *nasheed* concert to celebrate the *isra'* and *mi'raj*. I also saw a Hummer, which looked *really* out of place.

But more importantly, pizza was gooooooooooooooooooooood. And garlic bread was fantaaaaaaaastic.

I also stopped at the lobby and the souvenir shop was open. I ended up buying an English magazine titled *Yemen Today*, which was surprisingly very good. Not a patch on *Egypt Today* (where I work!) but good.

It's 1:30am now and we have an optional visit to a secluded beach right after Fajr. But - as the Brits here say - I'm 'knackered', so I'm not sure I'm going to be able to wake up after just two hours of sleep, but I will definitely try.

Day 33: Hamya

So today was another exhausting day in another city and here I was thinking we'd have so much free time I would be able to catch up on my memorisation of *Surah Yaseen*. But now I can barely keep my eyes open.

I did end up going to the beach this morning, only it turned out to be the exact same beach we went to a couple of days ago. It was a lot more crowded than it was at night, and windy, but on the plus side we could actually *see* the beach. And another good thing is that once the men in the area realised that there was a big group of women approaching, they kept their distance, and didn't automatically gravitate towards us.

We built a Tarimi mud house on the beach (pretty easy - just a big lump of sand) and a lot of us decided to actually swim which meant the bus driver wasn't really happy with us. We were supposed to have breakfast on the beach, which I was really looking forward to, but we couldn't because, and I quote, "There are too many men on the beach and it would be awkward for you to eat (with *niqab*)." I'm guessing he didn't realise everyone took their *niqab* off the second we got off the bus. Oops.

So we got back around 9am and were told to only have a quick shower because the bus was leaving at 10am. But of course we were running on AST (Arab Standard Time) and for some reason the men didn't show up before noon. And I'm the kind of person who can never sleep in public/on a bus/if it's noisy and (until I got here) if it's light so I was really exhausted.

We got to Hamya an hour and a half later, which is another city also by the coast. Its name is derived from the hot springs that fill the city.

Our first stop was at another school, named Batool (the one who worships a lot) after the Prophet's daughter Fatima al-Zahra ﷺ, who was also known as *al-batool*. We were all exhausted so we all kind of lay down for an hour or so, before lunching on (as is the norm) chicken and rice. But at least this chicken was more Moroccan-y, with spices. The best thing though was the dessert (which is usually bananas). The dessert was...drum roll please...ice-cream!

↑ *Hamya coastline with fishing boats*

We then made our way to the hot springs, which the Yemenis believe has *shifa'* (healing) properties - it's always hot and never dries up. The springs are located in one of the palm tree-filled valleys, so we finally got to visit one of them. And this one was especially unique because it was located directly on the beach; I felt like I was in a scene from *Lost*. The water was boiling hot (it literally scalded my hands) and smelled kind of eggy.

↑ *Palm trees at the springs in Hamya*

→ *Hot springs in Hamya*

After that we went to a *ribat* (combination library and mosque) to attend a lecture by Habib Umar. Unfortunately we were all so tired that at least half of us fell asleep, which I guess was ok since there was no translation which almost everyone needed.

After the lecture was over (just before Maghrib) we got on the bus to make our way over to the *mawlid* that was being held back in Makalla, but the majority of us were so tired the bus just took us back to our hotel.

Everyone was so tired and exhausted, but I'm guessing after relaxing in the air conditioned rooms and lying on the beds for a bit we felt better, because suddenly (and I can't believe this) everyone started prank-calling each other. Then we started getting hungry and ordered room service: spaghetti and chicken escalope and humus and tabbouleh and burgers and fries. Because even though our usual breakfast/sometimes dinner menu (*roti* (artisan) bread, chocolate spread, white cheese, jam) is good, it does get very repetitive, especially if you have it twice a day. And somehow, without planning it, we ended up having a mini party in our room.

And just as we were about to split up into our respective rooms, we got news that we would have a trip to a Yemeni *souk* (market) at around 10pm, after the brothers got home from a *walima* (feast) at a wedding (yes, they got invited and we didn't. Figures.). So we waited around for a couple of hours and then we were told that unfortunately the trip was cancelled because the men were late back.

So I'm ending today's entry by moaning about how much better the men have it. They got to chill in the pool this morning playing water polo while we had to swim in *abayas* and *hijab* on the beach; they have a shaykh with them so they can utilise their free time listening to lectures while we're stuck in a school doing nothing for a couple of hours; we get home and wait for a couple of hours for them to come back from a wedding feast; and our outing to the *souk* gets cancelled because of them. Alhamdulillah.

Today's Quote: "God gives the *dunya* (world) to who He loves and doesn't love, but only gives the *deen* (religion) to those He loves." (*Habib Umar*)

Day 34: Converts

Today was a relaxing day. We drove back to Tarim (stopping to buy coconuts on the way), slept until 'Asr, and then attended the *rawha* and the *mawlid* – it was especially bittersweet today because this is the last *mawlid* we will be attending.

↑ *Men selling coconuts at the side of the road*

It's wonderful to be back in Tarim, almost like going back home. It was especially nice going back to Dar al-Zahra and seeing all the Dar al-Zahra girls again. And it's such a small world – I ran into a girl there I had met two years ago in the *Litaarafuu* conference in Abu Dhabi following the cartoon crisis, who was in Tarim for a wedding.

On Thursdays after the *mawlid*, Habib Umar gives a small lecture, but there are also a number of guys who get up and give short five-minute lectures. Today, an American convert got up and gave a small lecture. Apparently he spoke before, but this is the first time I've heard him.

He talked about how he invited a US marine over to his home, who told him that killing people was a bigger rush than the heroin addiction he had as a child, which was so severe he tried to chew his way out of a wall when his parents locked him in a basement for six months to cure him.

The convert then explained how Islam gives him that rush, and how much he loves saying *la ilaha illa Allah* (there is no god but Allah). Then he pushed his sleeves up and showed us his tattoos, which were basically Hebrew letters, and told us that he used to be Jewish.

I love converts. I think that's been pretty clear when I've spoken about the three I've met here in this Dowra - Lara, Eva and Choclit. I love them even though so many of them are so zealous in the beginning (at least the ones I've met). I wish I was a convert. Not in the sense that I don't understand or appreciate the huge blessing I've been given to be born as a Muslim, but in the sense that converts appreciate the religion so much more. When you have a blessing for so long, you take it for granted - *ulf al ni'ma*.
It kind of reminds me of this woman I met in Makkah, who told me how lucky I was to not live there. "We see how much you appreciate the blessing of coming here," she told me, "while we rarely come simply because we live here and know that the Kabah is always here."

Today's Quote: "If you ask a pen why it writes, it'll tell you it's not in control, the fingers are. The fingers will tell you the hand is the one in control. The hand will tell you the arm is in control. The arm will tell you the body is in control. The body will tell you it's the heart that's in control, and the heart will tell you it isn't in control of the whims that take possession of it. The majority of people see the pen scratching on the surface of the planet and stop at that. Those with a little more knowledge may see the fingers." (*Habib Umar*)

Day 35: Back in Tarim

July is over, which means we have less than a week left before we have to go home. Our calendar is finally full. It's very, very sad. Being back in Tarim really feels like being back home - it felt so good to get back to our normal routine today.

Being back also brought back home the fact that your environment influences you more than you might realise. Makalla was our little test, taking us out of the spiritual bubble we were living in and I'm not too sure we all successfully passed.

Personally, I feel I didn't - I didn't pray Fajr two of the three mornings, even though I've only missed it three times this entire month (partial excuse was that we were all so exhausted, but that's not really an excuse); I gorged myself on mangoes and Pizza; I didn't keep up with my *awrad*, *and* I finally caved and listened to music on my iPhone, which I hadn't done in the entire month I've been here.

Tarim feels like a different world; it makes you want to be a better person. You're better not because you feel everyone is better so you imitate them blindly, but because Tarim somehow inexplicably gives you an extra drive - almost as if the very air is embodied with little spiritual 'infusions'. It sounds silly when I read it and I know I'm being repetitive, but it's true.

Here, I can get up at 3am, walk to Dar al-Zahra, sit for two hours for Tahajjud, Fajr and *awrad* until sunrise, which I couldn't even do in Makkah and definitely never even attempted back home. Back home, I'm lucky if I get up for Fajr and quickly do the normal *dhikr* we do after any prayer.

A big part of it is the fact that there's simply so little opportunity to be 'bad', in the sense that you're so isolated. If you're on a diet, it'll be easier if you're on a desert island than if you're living next to a KFC.

Which brings me to the thought: is seclusion really the better solution? There's no doubt that it's easier than being out in the world, and you will become a better person - whether you like it or not. But at the same time, I truly believe that seclusion only benefits you and no one else. If we're out in the world, it's true we'll have a harder time being 'good', but then we must get more 'ajr, reward, for staying away from temptations. Plus, we'll then be able to contribute to society, do da'wah and help others. To take what we've learnt and implement it in harder spiritual - if not physical - surroundings is better, especially since physical hardship is easier to deal with than spiritual hardship.

Today I got to try another delicious Yemeni salad - boiled potato cubes and tomato slices in a sauce made of water, sugar and a touch of *beesbas*.

Today we also got to pray behind Habib Kathim - he decided to keep going on after 'Isha so we could finish the section.

Today's Quote: "Don't sin and say: 'God will forgive me, He is Merciful and Forgiving.' Yes, He is, but don't be like the fisherman who sits on the shore and waits for a jewel to land in his lap. Yes, the sea is full of jewels but you have to go and seek them. So if you sin you need to seek forgiveness for your actions. You need to *shamar* (roll up your sleeves) and be diligent." (*Habib Kathim*)
Likewise:
"[Don't be] the man who wants to be learned in the sciences of religion but spends his time in idleness and says, 'God is generous and merciful, able to fill my heart with that knowledge with which He filled the hearts of His prophets and saints, without any effort on my part, any repetition, any learning from a teacher. Again, you resemble the man who wants wealth, yet does not engage in farming or commerce or any gainful occupation." (*Imam al-Ghazali*)

Day 36: Habib Kathim

Today Habib Kathim came over to the Dowra house for a two hour question and answer session. It was so good to finally 'see' him. It was even good to see the translator - we've been seeing the shaykhs and translators on TV for so long this kind of makes them 'real' people.

So it was only a Q & A session, but it felt like an intense *rawha* session simply because our teacher was sitting right in front of us: we concentrated more, we sat up, we focused on everything he was saying. Habib Kathim's mere presence affects our receptiveness to learn, if that makes sense. The men are so lucky. But we are still so lucky to have had the chance to learn from these amazing scholars. And they deserve all our respect. Prophet Muhammad ﷺ said:

"Honour scholars, as they are the inheritors of the prophets. Anyone who honours them has honoured Allah and His Messenger." (*Al-Khatib*)

Habib Kathim kept looking around at us, and it felt like he was looking directly at each one of us (we were all wearing *niqab* out of respect). He also kept smiling these little smiles. I wonder what he was thinking? We gave him our *sebah* (rosaries) to do *tasbeeh* with and give them back to us, and we got to pray 'Asr behind him. We also took pictures of him, which felt so rude and stupid to do (even though we can see flashing cameras through the curtains in class which means the men also take pictures).

So, the gist of Habib Kathim's advice/answers to our questions:

- You can increase your *iman* by increasing your acts of worship gradually, so you can sustain them. Pray on the Prophet. Read Qur'an. Read books about and by good people. They are small things but their effect is greater than you know.
- You do *istighfar* not just to erase your sins but to increase your rank with Allah.
- Good character is the best *da'wah*. It will be a magnet to other people.

- Just doing good deeds in front of those who don't, is *da'wah*.
- The key to having presence (*hudhoor*) in prayer is *wudu'* (ablution). When Imam al-Shafi'i died Sayyida Nafeesa (the granddaughter of al-Husayn, the Prophet's grandson) said, "May Allah have mercy on him, he perfected his *wudu'*." She said that and not "he was a great scholar," because if you perfect your *wudu'* it will lead to perfection in prayer and so on. Have presence and awareness in *wudu'* because it is the key to everything else.

And what made everyone smile:
To get married, recite Prophet Musa's 🕊 *du'a*,
"Rabbi anni lima anzalta ilayya min khayrin faqeer."
"My Lord! I am needy of whatever good Thou sendest down for me."
(Surat al-Qasas 28:24)

Habib Kathim also gave *bay'a* to about half a dozen of us who wanted to. He asked for those of us who didn't want to give it to get up and exit the room. It felt extremely rude to do that, kind of like saying, "I don't want to take *bay'a* with you," but I got up, and alhamdulillah, I wasn't the only one.

After Maghrib we had our class with him, and he gave us *ijaza* (permission [to transmit what has been taught]) as he ended. When he said it, I was doing *wudu'* in Habib Umar's house (which, by the way, was unlocked. Imagine leaving your door unlocked?) since we were going to pray 'Isha behind him. So now I have the memory of saying "*qabilt al-ijaza*" (I accept the *ijaza*) while doing *wudu'*!

Today was our last class with Habib Kathim and his last words to us were to make *du'a* when we saw the crescent, since tonight was the first night of Sha'ban, the month before Ramadan. Subhan Allah we had just left Habib Umar's house and looked up at the crescent and we felt a few drops of rain. Just small drops, almost insignificant, but rain. And then we saw the procession of men walking in the street chanting, "Hud, Hud, Hud" which they will do for the next seven nights until they leave for their visit to Prophet Hud ﷺ.

Today's Quote: "To attain the secret of knowledge, act upon it. To attain the secret of *dhikr,* do copious amounts of it. To attain the secret of prayer, have presence in it." (*Habib Kathim*)

Day 36 (Cont'd): Party

Well, I really don't know what to say. Other than the Danish/Swedish/Belgian group just swept *and* wiped the floor with us.

It's so hard to think of a way to convey the experience. If I write it like it was, "We sang *nasheeds* and ate," it sounds so mundane and the kind of thing that'll make people say: "ohhhhhh, okayyyyy then, rock on," before looking away and rolling their eyes at how boring that sounds. But it was so, so much fun. I know it seems silly to say it was a 'fulfilling' night, but that's what it was.

So we go to the Danish/Swedish/Belgian house, expecting that nothing they could do could top our night and the programme that we had prepared for them when they came to our house. But their hospitality put ours to shame.

So we sit and in front of every group is a plate of fruit, a plate of chips and a plate of cookies. Honestly, I thought that was the dinner, especially since one of them had told my roommate that they just had "snacks and tea".

And then the *nasheed* band walks in. Yes, they hired the female Tarimi *nasheed* band to entertain us. I don't know how it happened, but somehow almost everyone got up to dance and it was one of the strangest things ever. You had some dancing Tarimi style (kind of resembles the two step), some African style, some Kuwaiti style, and (most memorably) Eva's traditional Bulgarian dance.

As for food, what can I say? It's enough that they somehow managed to get us *burgers and chips* in Tarim. Yes, I know we got them pizza, but somehow burgers and chips in Tarim seems decadent. And that's not all - they went around with cookies, cakes, Twix cake (!), and actual chocolate bars. Not to mention constantly coming around with cold water and soft drinks. And tea in small Tarimi cups (where did they get them from?!) and in normal cups. And they had incense Tarimi style.

Truly, they were incredible hosts, miles better than us. And they were only about half a dozen people, while we were almost two dozen. They never sat down and kept coming around with new treats. I honestly felt like I was at a wedding and that of people I knew and loved.

Nasheeds are just as powerful as music and even more so because of the passion of the singers, which just emanates from their voices. It spurs you on, makes you clap harder and join in. *Nasheeds* give the gathering a sense of harmony and purpose - we're having fun and yet don't feel like we're wasting time. I know I'm not explaining it properly, but I guess you had to be there.

So we walked home at around midnight trying to console ourselves by saying that we only had five hours to prepare for their party while they had days to prepare for theirs and that they were all 'Arabs' so had the hospitality gene in them. Never mind that most of them were born in their respective countries even if their parents were originally Arab. (And that excuse doesn't work with me because I am 'Arab' (actually African, but whatever).)

Its 2:50am now and there's Tahajjud in ten minutes. I was thinking of skipping it then remembered what I heard this week: the true student of knowledge is as prepared on the last day of classes as he was on the first. Guess I'm pulling an all-nighter.

Today's Quote: "No one comes to *ma'idat al-rahman* (charity tables that are set out in Ramdan at *iftar* time for anyone to come and eat) because they want to - they come because Allah wants them to come. Likewise, we have been gathered here in Tarim together because Allah wants us to come." (*Um Suffian, the Danish/Swedish/Belgian group leader*)

Day 37: Final Reflections on Classes

Tahajjud: This isn't really a class, but part of the Dowra experience that I really enjoyed and wish I'd taken better advantage of. But because we pray Tahajjud in the Dowra house, I only actually attended Tahajjud in Dar al-Zahra in my first and last week. And that's embarrassing to admit because there are some of us who attend as often as they can to listen to the *awrad*, and - this is the embarrassing bit - they don't even speak Arabic! If I didn't speak or understand Arabic I'd probably just fall asleep or not bother to get up in the first place except to pray.

But Tahajjud in Dar al-Zahra is such a communal, sharing experience that time flies by. It is so, so hard back home to wake up for ten minutes to pray Fajr and I can press the snooze button on my alarm every five minutes for a whole hour because I'm too tired to get up. But it's so much easier here.

Part of it is because they read the *awrad* together (I think the *Khulasa* (the *awrad* book) is my best friend now) and so you feel like you're doing something constructive with the time, and not just sitting there aimlessly for half an hour thinking, "Ok, I prayed my Tahajjud, what *du'a* should I make now?" And because you're doing it together there's much less chance of you stopping halfway through or daydreaming or losing concentration. It gives you added incentive to do the *awrad*, especially since they're on the radio - you can just turn it on after every prayer and recite them. Plus they do it in a sing song voice so it's not just monotonously reading from a book. I am going to miss that voice a lot, I know I will.

Even walking to and from Dar al-Zahra for Tahajjud is a good experience - you get to reflect in the silent darkness on the way there, and enjoy the sunrise, good weather, and rooster crowing on your way back. Plus of course you get '*ajr* for every step you take.

I think I've spent more time in the *musallah* in Dar al-Zahra praying, doing *awrad*, memorising Qur'an etc., than I have in any time I've been to the *Haram* in Makkah, subhan Allah.

I will really miss it here. Most of all, I will miss the *musafaha*, the Dar al-Zahra girls and the comforting, Indonesian (slightly nasal sounding), "Astaghfiru Allahhhhhh, astaghfiru Allahhhhhh, astaghfiru Allahhhhhhh."

Tajweed/Qur'an memorisation: Our teacher was really, really good mash'Allah, and even though I've been reciting and memorising Qur'an for years she caught me on a number of things I do wrong when I recite, which insha'Allah I'm going to work hard to correct. Basically we went over *tajweed* rules and recited to her once a week.

Again, this class makes me thank Allah so much for the blessing of Arabic. So much of the *tajweed* rules I knew instinctively because I speak Arabic, while I could see others who didn't know struggling with the pronunciation. Alhamdulillah.

Alhamdulillah, I managed to memorise *Surah Yaseen* and a quarter of *Surat al-Kahf*, which I'm planning to finish, insha'Allah, when I get back. I think this class is particularly good for Westerners who might not have as easy access to good Qur'an teachers in the West. But since alhamdulillah, I do, I kind of wish we didn't have this class three times a week and instead took another class that we can't study as easily in our countries with teachers who are as qualified.

Fiqh: I love our teacher, mash'Allah, he's funny, interactive, and most of all - acknowledges the fact that there are women there too! But unfortunately, we only covered purification and a little bit of prayer. It's good because you realise how vast knowledge is, how little you know and how much you have to learn, but bad because we haven't covered as much.

It's weird to realise that almost all of our class textbooks are just small booklets. The *fiqh* class book is an A5 sized thirty-three page booklet, *The Lives of Man* is only seventy something pages, and the Divine Unity book is the tiniest of all - in Arabic it's literally a pocket sized (or actually more like the size of half your palm) twelve page booklet.

Al-Rawha: What can I say about the *rawha*? Just that it's truly a class that makes you feel like the most worthless person in the world. This class makes me feel ten times worse than I did when I read Shaykh Hamza Yusuf's *Purification of the Heart*, or studied a similar class with him during the Rihla.

The only drawback about this class is that it's too spiritually high (for me). I feel like I have a long way to go before I can even *attempt* to address the issues Habib Umar is speaking about. Like, for example, he was saying today: "If you were offered the chance to be the king of the entire world from the beginning to the end of the time and your heart is moved at all by that, then your heart isn't pure enough." As if. Here's me still struggling with not gossiping and you're talking about the purest, purest heart. As my housemate Masooma says: "We still need to be potty trained."

But one thing that struck me particularly in the *rawha* is how much the book we're studying mentions *'al-Ethar'*. I asked those who listened to the translation how it was translated and they said as 'preference', but of course that doesn't convey the entire meaning. So yes, it struck me because of course that's my name, and it made me realise what an important thing it is to have. So I'm working on that.

The Beginning of Guidance: This is my favourite class. I realised a couple of weeks ago that I've actually had this book for years when I saw an identical copy to mine in Dar al-Zahra (in Arabic). The Arabic version is pocket book sized and it's one of those books I picked up somewhere that's sitting on a shelf which I'm going to read 'one day'.

So subhan Allah, like one of my housemates believes, "If you're meant to get knowledge, you'll get it when it's time." So maybe I wouldn't have identified as much with the book as I have now in this stage of my life. I loved this class because I feel, unlike the *rawha*, that some of the things we're studying are actually within my reach - like trying to not lie, backbite etc.

Da'wah in the West: Habib Ali is incredible, mash'Allah. You would never think that someone as 'traditional' as he was could have so much insight and understanding towards the issues Muslims in the West face. And even though Habib Ali was only here for about two weeks worth of classes, we still learned a lot.

Da'wah: I really *loved* this class. Habib Ali really hit the nail on the head - he went through all the obstacles Muslims face when attempting to do *da'wah*, and then went through PowerPoint presentations describing how best to go about it.

Hadith: I loved this class. It's the only one where we almost covered all the material (probably because it was the only one in English so we didn't lose half the time in translation), and I've learned so much from it.

The Lives of Man: I love all of Imam al-Haddad's books (and I really recommend everyone read them, most have been translated), and studying this book with Habib Umar has been great - I've read it twice before and yet I've learned things in our class that I never even thought of. I wish we could have covered all five stages though (we only managed to cover the first two).

Tawheed: A vital course everyone needs to study, because the world we live in today is one of bewildering spiritual and intellectual confusion. As Sheikh Hamza Yusuf mentioned in one of his books, "The purpose of Islam is to teach humanity unity. It begins with the unity of our Lord, that we unify Him in our understanding."

Seerah: Listening to the Prophet's biography will always be beautiful, no matter how many times I listen to it.

I've learned so much on this Dowra. But again, I've learned so much more out of class than in it, more from the people and the place than from the books.

Today I went to the bookstore and the supermarket with my brother. And this is going to sound really sad, but I had a lot of fun. I guess deprivation makes the most mundane things fun. Apparently, the Yemeni alternative to Red Bull is 'Sharks'.

Today we were also invited for dinner in someone's mansion, complete with swimming pool and pool tables.

Today's Quote: "Staying away from the *dunya* doesn't mean secluding yourself. It means, like a scholar once said, 'Have the *dunya* in your hand, and not your heart. The new *dhikr* of our time is monitoring stocks twenty-four hours [a day]. Do business, be a millionaire, but don't have the *dunya* in your heart. Don't let money control you - you must control it." (*Shaykh Imaad*)

Day 38: Muslim While Flying

We found a huge scorpion-looking bug in our room today, with two strange suction looking things at its head. I will definitely not miss the bugs here, especially the fat looking ants.

Today was technically the last day of classes and it felt very strange to know that, especially since we are in no way close to finishing the assigned texts in most of the classes.

In *fiqh* class today one of the brothers brought up a very interesting topic: 'Muslim while flying'. Somehow I never realised how hard it must be to be constantly looked at with a suspicious eye simply because you're a Muslim. The brother who spoke talked about how the flight attendant wouldn't even look at him when he wanted 7Up, and how frightened she was when he tried to go to the bathroom during turbulence. It's sad how the media has managed to paint Muslims as the enemy. I wish I could somehow hold Tarim up and say, "This is what Islam is, this is what its followers should be doing. What you see is not Islam."

We then had an optional question and answer session with our *fiqh* teacher and he asked us all to think hard about what we will take back with us from Tarim.

After 'Asr we finished *adab al-nufoos*, the book we are studying in the *rawha*, and Habib Umar gave us all *ijaza* in teaching it. Alhamdulillah, I managed to buy the CDs of the entire *rawha* so I can re-listen to them back home. I feel bad for the Westerners since they were only available in Arabic.

After Maghrib we had a surprise - Habib Ali was back. He left a week ago to go to Yale University in America for the first follow up conference of *A Common Word*, and we had been told he most probably wouldn't be back for the end of the Dowra. So it was a welcome surprise when he saw him. The session was a question and answer session, and it had one added benefit - the women had a microphone and were allowed to ask their questions (gasp) out LOUD. Kudos to Habib Ali.

He told us a story in answer to a question and it was about Habib Umar and his *ethar*:
Some Indonesian students came to study in Tarim in a winter back when the facilities weren't as complete and they complained to Habib Umar that they didn't have blankets. So Habib Umar went inside his house and came back with blankets. They said they weren't enough so he went back and brought more. They told him there was one more student without a blanket so he went back, stayed a very, very long time and eventually came back with a blanket that didn't smell very nice.

The next day, the Indonesian students were told by someone who worked in Habib Umar's house, "Do you know what happened in Habib Umar's house yesterday? You wanted blankets so he gave you his and his wife's blanket. You wanted more, he gave you his daughters' blankets. You wanted one more and he could only find the blanket of his baby son, which is why it didn't smell very nice."

This was at a time when Habib Umar didn't have enough money to create duplicate copies of his tapes, let alone buy new blankets. Habib Ali then ended the story by telling us that he wasn't telling us a story of scholars gone by, but of someone in our lifetimes.

Al-Ethar is a beautiful thing.

Today's Quote: "Falsehoods spread with money and wealth, truth with sacrifice. *Da'wah* isn't a bed of roses, you should expect it to be hard." (*Habib Ali*)

Day 39: One Day Left

There was *bay'a* with Habib Umar today - those of us who did it got to hold on to his shawl (which apparently smelt beautiful).

There are no more classes scheduled, so from sunrise to 'Asr we did nothing because the electricity was out and none of us could summon the energy to do anything. The electricity has been crazy all week, and we've been stuck without AC for a couple of hours at least twice this week - thank goodness for the mulan-style fans, I think they're the best thing we bought!

Today we also attended a *hadra* (gathering) after 'Asr, where we basically recite a number of *qaseedas*. Habib Umar's wife then gave a small lecture about the benefits of *dhikr* and doing *salawat* on Prophet Muhammad ﷺ.

There were women selling stuff there so I ended up buying one of the Tarimi straw baskets they put *heef* in. In Egypt we eat *baladi* bread which is also big and round so it's perfect. I also bought some Tarimi straw hand-held brooms - as souvenirs, of course! And of course some of the great Tarimi cupcakes (they put *heel* (cardamom) in them which gives them a really great taste) and Tarimi mint.

Today the ring I had ordered also arrived, it's a really pretty one with Prophet Muhammad's ﷺ seal imprinted in it.

After Maghrib was the Dowra's closing ceremony in Dar al-Mustafa and it was packed. We could see (on TV of course) men sitting in the doorway and beyond. It was a really beautiful two hour programme. *Qaseedas* were recited, including Imam al-Haddad's that we studied in the *rawha*, and then some men got up to recite things they had memorised from their shar'iah books. Young boys recited some ahadith, and others the *du'a* you make when you leave the house. Other men got up and said the most important thing they learned from the Dowra. So basically, snippets of what they'd learned.

Then two men from the English Dowra spoke, and one of them said he couldn't understand his wife's longing to come here, and only understood it when he came. That's so true - unless you come here, you won't know what you've been missing. Like he said, Tarim represents everything Islam stands for, and here you feel that every single person is better than you. If you find yourself weakening and getting engrossed in the *dunya* when you get back, he advised, all you have to do is close your eyes and remember everyone you've met here.

Another British guy then spoke (a lot of British people come here by the way because the *habayeb* visit England a lot more often than they do the States) and said how incredible it was to sit with people who have seen faces who have seen faces who have seen faces who have seen the Prophet Muhammad ﷺ.

Then a lot of different men spoke - one recited some slightly peculiar poetry, one Egyptian (go Egypt!) gave advice, one was Tanzanian etc. One scholar (I think his name was al-Shattery) said that if we leave here having memorised Imam al-Haddad's *qaseeda* and implement it in our lives, then that would be more than enough.

Finally, the night ended with Habib Ali and Habib Umar speaking.

Today's Quote: "People are sick of *kalam* [talk] and they won't listen to it anymore. We don't need people who talk anymore, we need people who act, and who do *da'wah* through their character and behaviour, not their speech." (*Habib Ali*)

Day 39 (Cont'd): Wrapping Up

There's only one more day to go. It's time to write down my resolutions before I go back and get sucked back into the 'real' world.

Being here in Tarim, I've given up a lot of stuff cold turkey - beds, fast food, Facebook, driving, pleasure reading, TV, music, clothes, mirrors etc. And there's a whole lot of other stuff which I've almost given up cold turkey like soft drinks, chocolate and the internet.

It's weird in a good way to not have all that stuff, but it's been a lot easier than I thought to not have it. Don't get me wrong, the second I'm on the plane I'm taking off my *niqab*, having a fast food feast and spending a day on Facebook and another day sleeping, but I know that in a day or two I'll have satiated the desire for all the things I'm looking forward to, and that after a couple of days they're not going to be all that. So even though I'm looking forward to going back I'm not *desperately* looking forward to it.

(Note: I have the utmost respect for *niqabis*, but *niqab* just isn't for me. But this experience has made me respect *niqabis* a lot more than I used to, and has given me a more open mind about what it entails to wear it. I don't dislike it as much as I used to.)

I know myself, and I know that if I don't make some concrete resolutions to stick up on my wall, I might forget all my good intentions. Character wise, there's a whole list of things I'm hoping to implement, but basically it boils down to me needing to think more before I speak, and to treat my family the way I do friends.

As for the 'outward' acts:

- Never miss Fajr prayer. Get up for Tahajjud at least during the weekend. It's Sunnah and as Shaykh Imaad says, "Sunnah acts protects the *fard*." i.e. if you do Sunnah, then when you get lazy you'll just skip it. But if you don't do it, then when you get lazy you'll skip the *fard*.

- Keep up with my *awrad* - the bare minimum is the *wird al–latif*, which insha'Allah I will learn by heart. Keep the *khulasa* with me everywhere I go.

- Use the *siwak* as often as I can.

- Say "Salam alaykum" when I answer the phone.

- Stop to listen to the *adhan*. I live in the city of a thousand minarets, I have no excuse not to.

- Finish reading Imam al-Ghazali's *Ihya' Ulum ad-Din* (Revival of the Religious Sciences).

- Create a whole load of *nasheed* playlists. My room supervisor so very kindly allowed me to copy 12 GB worth of *nasheeds* and lectures from her computer, so again, I have no excuse.

- Go back and review/re-memorise all the Qur'an *surahs* (chapters) I memorised as a child. Read at least a *hizb* (2.5 pages) of Qur'an a day.

- Read at least one Arabic book a fortnight.

They may not seem like 'big' changes, but as Imam al-Halabi
said:
"To do a thing today, and the same tomorrow,
Gathering is the essence of knowledge.
This one may achieve wisdom,
For a stream is but the gathering of drops."

In the end, I want to leave, not from Tarim, but *with* Tarim.

Day 40: Our Last Day

It feels weird to write about today just like it's any other day. It still hasn't sunk
in that today is really our last day. And I don't want to think about it so I'll just
talk about today like it was any other day.

Today I went through another lesson in patience: I got stuck
outside Dar al-Zahra from 3:20 until 4am, which meant I basically
missed Tahajjud (though I turned on my radio and did my *awrad*
outside). We were stuck outside because apparently they couldn't
find the woman who has the key. (They lock the doors at night and
I'm assuming the key changes rooms/women who keep it every
night.) Patience is definitely something I have to work on.

Anyway, after dawn lots of men from Dar al-Mustafa spoke
about the end of the Dowra and what it means to them for
about an hour.

The Jewish convert spoke again and this time about *da'wah*. And
subhan Allah he was incredible; he says he was so joyful with
Islam that he literally took a road trip from New York to California
to talk to people on his way about Islam. He went right up to a
man at a gas station and asked him if he knew about the Day of
Judgement. He went up to a man in a doctor's office. Both of
them took *shahada* at his hands and converted to Islam.

I can't understand the bravery of going up to people and initiating a discussion about Islam, especially when they didn't ask, or worse, if you don't know them. The Jewish convert says he gives *da'wah* to everyone, even a police officer who once pulled him over for speeding.

He reminded me of Fadel Soliman, the president of Bridges Foundation. When I was doing the first stage of Dr. Soliman's Public Presenters for Peace (PPP) programme, which is how to present Islam to non-Muslims, he told us a story to illustrate how important it is to give *da'wah* to everyone:

"I was on a plane in the US and it was a four hour flight. I asked the woman sitting next to me if she wanted to listen to a presentation about Islam. She said no. I told her, 'How about you listen to it and I give you $100 if you don't learn anything?' She said ok. So I gave her the presentation. I asked her if she wanted the money, and she said no."

For me, speaking to non-practicing Muslims about Islam is hard, let alone to non Muslims. Religion is just such a sensitive topic and it's just so awkward. But imagine the reward if you do it and manage to change a misconception or stereotype.

Anyway, half an hour after the *awrad* finished we got on a bus to visit some of the mosques in Tarim, which boasts over 365. I was thinking of not going since I'd only had two hours of sleep, but I am *so* glad I went.

The bus dropped us off in the Ba 'Alawi square, known as the heart of Tarim.

↑ *Mosque in the Ba 'Alawi square*

Our first stop was the Ba 'Alawi mosque, built by Faqih al-Muqaddam's grandson. I prayed in the area he used to pray in.

↑ *Door to the mosque of Ba 'Alawi*

↑ *Minaret of the mosque of Ba 'Alawi*

Then we went to the mosque of Abu Qader al-Saqqaf, who wanted to marry Shaykha Sultana.

This was followed by a visit to the mosque of Muhammad (Sa'ad) bin 'Alawi al-'Aidrus and I prayed in his *khalwa* (seclusion/worship) area. It was seriously creepy - the room (if you can call it that) is basically a hole in the ground, and when I put my elbows out I touch the sides. The ceiling is ten centimetres above my head, and you can't lie down in it. I was there for ten minutes and felt claustrophobic, how could he stand to be there for so long? It's definitely coffin-like and I'm guessing reminded him of being in the grave one day.

↑ *Mosque of Muhammad
bin 'Alawi al-'Aidrus*

→ *Khalwa area of Muhammad
bin 'Alawi al-'Aidrus*

↓ *Minaret of Omar al-Saqqaf
(al-Mihdar) mosque*

Our last stop of the morning was the mosque of Omar al-Saqqaf, the son of Abu Qader al-Saqqaf. He's known as Omar al-Mihdar (the present) though, because of his 'presence', and his daughter 'Aisha is buried there. The mosque is huge, and has a 150 metre-high minaret - the tallest mud minaret in the world.

The *wudu'* areas in the mosque are split up into tiny rooms, and each one has a steep well full of water for *ghusl* (kind of like the ones in the Afghani *Osama* movie. Osama was the name of the girl hero, not *that* Osama). I had a quick dip and it was surprisingly cool and refreshing.

↑ *Ablution areas in the mosque of Omar al-Saqqaf*

↑ *Standing at the stage across from the mosque of Omar al-Saqqaf, where the mahaba awards were once held*

After 'Asr was the *khatm* (closing) for women in Habib Umar's courtyard and it was so, so packed. It was similar to Dar al-Mustafa's, minus the speeches. Habib Ali's daughter (she's nine) gave a little lecture and mash'Allah her mannerisms are exactly like her dad's, a scholar in the making.

After 'Isha we visited Zambal again, which was a great opportunity since last time we didn't really get a chance to properly visit as it had been so late.

We're all just chilling now in a room, eating all the leftover cookies and crackers I bought when I went to the supermarket with my brother a while back. We asked a *henna* woman to come over and I just had henna done. It took almost two hours to do the front and back of my hands and arms up to my elbows, but it's so beautiful - a fitting way to celebrate my time in Tarim.

Tahajjud is in forty minutes, so we're going to spend the time until then up on the roof, one last time. I can't believe I'm leaving in twelve hours. It seems so surreal and it hasn't really hit me that I have to get up and pack now, and that this is my last night on this mattress, in this house, up on that roof staring at those mountains.

↓ *Valleys full of water outside Tarim a day after rainfall*

It rained buckets today - it's only rained that way once since I've been here, at the twenty day mark. It's wonderful to walk in the rain and breeze. They say *du'a* is accepted when it rains, that the doors of the sky are opened. So my *du'a* is: To come back to Tarim one day, insha'Allah.

Day 40 (Cont'd): Leaving Tarim

I know that technically this is day 41, but since I didn't sleep last night I'm just going to continue with day 40 so I can stick to the title of 40 days.

So we went up on the roof at 2:30am and it began to rain slightly. It was beautiful to walk to Dar al-Zahra in the cool weather and feel the rain drops on my face (I took off the *niqab* - no one is in the streets at that time). Only it turns out the electricity was out and it was pitch black in Dar al-Zahra and stifling with no AC. My small portable radio came to the rescue and we could listen to the *awrad*. It was a surreal experience to be in the dark reciting the *awrad*. Though at the same time without the distraction of the lights, the sound of the AC, and people around you, it kind of boiled the experience down to the bare bones of what it's supposed to be: just you trying to connect with Allah.

After Fajr was a *mawlid*, a series of small lectures and *qaseeda* recitations. We then had our final *musafaha*, only this time it was *musafahat al-wada'* (farewell), where you literally hugged every single Dar al-Zahra student, kissed their hand, and asked for their forgiveness and *du'a*. I'm not a huggy person and I dithered for ages before finally joining the line as the last person since I knew it would take so long, but subhan Allah it was a beautiful experience. Girls I only knew by 'face' cried as they hugged me and I truly felt like I'd miss them. And other than the fact that my back and knees hurt from bending down to hug them (it seems every single Dar al-Zahra girl is short compared to me), I am so glad I went.

I then made my way back to the Dowra house and after a whirlwind of packing, we sat down for our last 'meeting' in our communal room. Some *hababas* were there, as well as women from the Dowra administration who had helped organise our incredible stay here.

We were each given small gifts (mine was a pretty incense kit) and a copy of all the Dowra lectures in English for free, which is truly the best gift of all. We were also given certificates of participation in the Dowra, and it was the first time certificates have even been given for the English Dowra participants. The certificates said:

The administration of Dar al-Mustafa for Islamic studies recognizes the participation of [name] from [country] who attended the summer intensive that was held from 1/7/2008 until 6/8/2008 of the Gregorian calendar, which coincided with the 27th of Jamad al-Akbar until the 5th of Sha'ban 1429 Hijri during which they received lessons in various Islamic sciences including jurisprudence, theology, Hadith methodology and transmission, as well as Qur'anic science. This certification should also serve to remind said student to remain God conscious and to work towards the embodiment of the characteristics and mannerisms of the Prophet Muhammad, may Allah's peace and blessings be upon him. We also advise that they continue studying these sciences as well as teaching others and implementing that which they were taught. Habib Umar.

We then had a little programme to thank our supervisors, and above all, our wonderful wonder, Ustadha Moneeba. I have learned *so* much from her and I am going to miss her so much. We sang her a song to the tune of Zain Bhika's *I think my mum is amazing* that one of us rewrote the lyrics to, so it read, "I think my *mushrifa* is amazing." Seriously, I don't think there was a dry eye in the house.

And so after a lot of hugging and furiously writing notes in each other's notebooks we made our way over to the Seiyun airport, which is literally the size of a large room. There was a European woman there dressed in a miniskirt and tank top, and it was very disconcerting to see - almost like culture shock.

An hour later we were in Sanaa and the luxury of a hotel room (a real, real hotel) seems so, so, so decadent. I know that in a couple of days I'll automatically adjust again, and won't even think of it, but now the luxury of a fully equipped bathroom with marble floors and chocolates on my pillow just felt strange. On the plus side, the beautiful weather in Sanaa feels like a gift - for me the weather is like Egyptian winter.

After 'Isha, we then had an amazing opportunity: to sit with Habib Ali (who had just landed in Sanaa) for a two hour question and answer session. Now *that's* a fitting ending to the Dowra.

And that's it.

Dubai

It's back to the *dunya* and nowhere epitomises the *dunya* more than Dubai, where I've just spent the last couple of days.

→ *Emirates Towers, Dubai*

Tarim and Dubai aren't just on opposite sides of the spectrum, they're on completely different planets. And to go from one extreme to the other has been more difficult than I could have imagined, being thrust into everything we've been so far away from for weeks and weeks. Even the view around me is aesthetically distressing - imagine going from seeing mud houses to seeing Burj Dubai, the tallest building in the world. Other than the moon, absolutely nothing is the same.

I have Tarim withdrawal symptoms.

I can't get over how much *stuff* is around us. I've got so used to subsisting on so very little - and I proved to myself that it's possible to do so - so everything just seems like such an extravagance, and all the *stuff* that seems so necessary just seems superfluous. There are four mirrors in my hotel room and I find myself just looking around at them, bewildered at their uselessness. Why do I need four mirrors?

I spent my first day in Dubai with an uneasy feeling in the pit of my stomach. Not butterflies, but more like a rock. I spent half the day sleeping and woke up feeling uncomfortable, like there was something important I had to do that I had forgotten, or like I had lost something. It seems strange to be doing nothing.

Physically, I couldn't be better. The first thing I did when I got to the hotel was order room service and did I enjoy my steak with French fries. And dessert. Then I slept on the poofy pillows in the divinely comfortable hotel bed. Waking up when my body wanted to wake up was pure bliss.

But emotionally, I feel torn. I can't bring myself to shop and when I did eventually drag myself to a mall, I couldn't help myself from just watching people around me. I felt that I was looking at them from far away, and that everyone scurrying around was failing miserably at seeing the bigger picture, like ants who cannot comprehend the universe around them.

Dubai is a life of heedlessness. The word soul-sucking is perfect for it. The people here have every material thing they could possibly dream of - I even saw an advert for a 24-carat gold facial! - and yet they're still not happy. They're still unfulfilled and striving to fill a gaping hole in their souls which many cannot comprehend. Contrast that with the people of Tarim, whose faces are aglow with spiritual contentment and I just feel all the more depressed.

Oh sure, I had fun with my Dowra sisters who were also here in Dubai for a few days. We went to the movies, stayed up all night talking and enjoyed our caramel popcorn, Krispy Kreme doughnuts and room service. So I'm happy in a sense, but being plunged into an ocean of materialism with no buffer leaves me adrift in confusion.

Because of the way I was living, it seems like I have crystal clear vision. I can laugh now at the branded sunglasses and bags, looking straight through them as the pathetic displays of ostentation they are. I passed through Harvey Nichols and I was tempted by nothing. I can see the materialism driven world we live in for the sham it is. But will my eyesight be so clear in a year? In a month even? How quickly will I slip back into my normal life and into my 'normal' way of thinking?

Egypt

I'm back in Cairo.

↑ *Sphinx and the Pyramids, Cairo*

It feels so good to be home. To breathe in the polluted air, to be out in the gridlocked streets, and to become one of the eighty million that inhabit this country. It's so good to see the rest of my family and, more importantly, sleep in my bed!

Getting back to 'normal' life feels strange, almost as if my life had been on hold for six years rather than six weeks. It feels strange to wear a different pair of shoes, considering the fact that I've been wearing the same pair for six weeks. It's strange to drive my car, to go off and run errands that are so not constructive - I mean, I know they're necessary, but they don't seem vital.

It's the middle of August which means this is the hottest it's going to get, and yet I feel like I'm in Spring. After Tarim, I don't think I'm ever going to think Egypt is hot again.

I'm off to the beach.

Beach

It's gorgeously idyllic. I've just spent a weekend doing absolutely nothing. A day swimming in the pool and a day swimming in the sea. A night sleeping till noon and a night lying on a hammock trying to make out the summer triangle constellation.

I know that I deserve a weekend off before I go back to work tomorrow, and that this weekend is basically my holiday, but I can't get over the fact that Tarim seems so, so far at this moment. Looking at the palm trees in the garden is like pressing on a bruise near my heart.

↑ *Beach – View from my house on the North Coast*

Summer in Egypt is the time of bumming around and literally doing absolutely nothing other than having fun. People wake up at noon, spend all day at the beach, and then all night chilling, not going to bed before dawn.

Being on the north coast in the summer, seeing everyone dressed so revealingly was honestly a kind of shock. After living with people with so much modesty it just seems so crude to be walking around half naked. So much flaunting of the flesh, and honestly it makes me despair about how low we've sunk and how far we have to go if we want to get ourselves out of this pit we've dug ourselves into.

On the (all female) beach, I had fun. But once I found myself singing along about them apple bottom jeans and beautiful liars along with the DJ, I had to take a step back. It's so easy to get sucked back into everything you say you want to stay away from. But this is the period where I have to be strongest, where I have to formulate the habits I want to keep. I don't want to slip back into my normal life; I don't want to have the incredible experience of Tarim register as no more than a blip on the radar of my life.

The lives of (most) people in the social circles I'm part of are fake and hollow. Oh yes, they're definitely glittering and extravagant, but they're empty. We were invited yesterday to one of the 'social gatherings' my family frequents, and it got to a point where I couldn't take it anymore. The gossiping, the aimless conversation that was absolutely devoid of purpose, the fake laughter and the vapidity of it all got to me.

So I took off to sit outside and look at the water, only to hear pounding stereo music in the distance. Like I said I would, I miss the silence of Tarim.

Eventually we left at 2:30 in the morning only to get stuck for an hour in traffic on the way back (and this is a highway) because of a concert Egypt's most famous singer (Amr Diab) was giving.

And this was the night of the 15th of Sha'ban.

I'm laughing on the outside, having fun with my family and friends, but on the inside I feel off-kilter. Tarim seems like it was a million miles away and I miss almost everything about it. I want to hold on to it but with every passing day it gets further away. It's like holding on to a dream when you wake up, or like Bastian in the Never Ending story trying to hold on to his memories. If Tarim was a well I took water from, then it's like trying to hold on to that water which I've simply cupped in my hand. My Yemeni housedress has become my security blanket, but I can't hold on to it forever.

I find myself thinking to myself: did it really happen? Did I just spend forty days of my life in one of the purest places I will ever visit? A place where you feel the entire universe *conspires* to help you be the best you could possibly be?

I just had a big Egyptian breakfast with my family and then the indulgence of eating grapes while sitting on a bar stool in the pool. I can hear the waves crashing on the beach and I have the sun on my face and a breeze on my back. Insha'Allah I'm going to go have a seafood dinner tonight while watching the beautiful sunset on a shore in Alexandria. I'm happy.

But would you believe I was happier trudging to Dar al-Zahra in the blazing heat dressed in black from head to toe and getting by on three hours of sleep? Perhaps it was a different kind of happiness, but it was definitely a more 'full-bodied' happiness, a richer kind.

Tomorrow I go back to work and the real, real world.

This will be my last entry. I think I've fulfilled the request that I write some of my reflections after my return and any more will just be dragging out the inevitable: that things have to come to an end sooner or later.

Today there's going to be a lunar eclipse. They say *du'a* is accepted then. So my *du'a* today, as it was on the last day of the Dowra when it rained, is to go back to Tarim one day. I said once that I wanted Tarim to come back *with* me. Today I'll add on to that: I hope that Tarim came back with me and that it will *stay* with me.

↑ *Sunset over a mountain in Tarim*

Ya rab.

Ya rab.

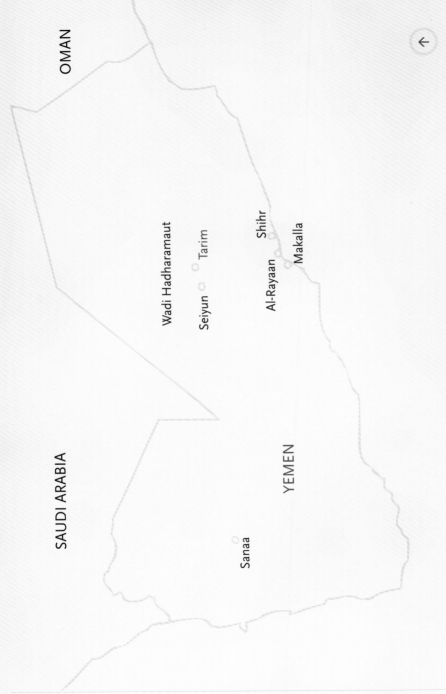

OMAN

SAUDI ARABIA

Wadi Hadharamaut

Seiyun ○ ○ Tarim

Shihr

Al-Rayaan

Makalla

YEMEN

Sanaa ○

Notes